British Muslims
Loyalty and Belonging

Proceedings of a sem~~inar held~~ ~~~~of CHESTER C~~~~

Edited by
Mohammad Siddique Seddon,
Dilwar Hussain *and* Nadeem Malik

THE ISLAMIC FOUNDATION
&
THE CITIZEN ORGANISING FOUNDATION

Published by

THE ISLAMIC FOUNDATION

Markfield Conference Centre
Ratby Lane, Markfield
Leicestershire LE67 9SY, United Kingdom
Tel: 01530 244944/5, Fax: 01530 244946
E-mail: i.foundation@islamic-foundation.org.uk
Website: www.islamic-foundation.org.uk

Quran House, P.O. Box 30611, Nairobi, Kenya

P.M.B. 3193, Kano, Nigeria

THE CITIZEN ORGANISING FOUNDATION
112 Cavell Street
London E1 2JA
Tel: 020 7375 1658, Fax: 020 7375 2034
Website: www.cof.org.uk

British Library Cataloguing-in-Publication Data

British Muslims: Loyalty and Belonging
   1. Muslims - Great Britain - Attitudes 2. Identity
(Psychology) - Great Britain - Religious aspects - Islam
   3. Muslims - Great Britain - Political activity 4. Allegiance
- Great Britain
   I. Seddon, Mohammad Siddique II. Hussain, Dilwar III. Malik,
Nadeem IV. Islamic Foundation
   305.6'971'041

ISBN 0 86037 308 8

Printed in Great Britain by Antony Rowe Ltd, Chippenham, Wiltshire

Cover/Book design & typeset: Nasir Cadir

Contents

Transliteration Table

Consonants. Arabic

initial: unexpressed medial and final:

ء	'	د	d	ض	ḍ	ك	k
ب	b	ذ	dh	ط	ṭ	ل	l
ت	t	ر	r	ظ	ẓ	م	m
ث	th	ز	z	ع	'	ن	n
ج	j	س	s	غ	gh	هـ	h
ح	ḥ	ش	sh	ف	f	و	w
خ	kh	ص	ṣ	ق	q	ي	y

Vowels, diphthongs, etc.

Short: ـَ a   ـِ i   ـُ u

long: ـَا ā   ـُو ū   ـِي ī

diphthongs: ـَوْ aw

                 ـَىْ ay

Preface

This publication is the product of the seminar, *British Muslims: Loyalty and Belonging*, which took place at the Markfield Conference Centre on the 8th of May 2002. It was organised as a joint programme between The Islamic Foundation and The Citizen Organising Foundation to address a number of pertinent issues relating to the current status of British Muslims who are under increasing public scrutiny in expressed terms of their allegiances and loyalties. To some extent this is, of course, revisited territory and echoes popular sentiments voiced during the *Satanic Verses* affair and the Gulf War. Muslim dissent to these events has been interpreted as disloyalty and a misplaced sense of belonging rather than a democratic right to express opposition. In addition, the apparent unwillingness of the Muslim community to assimilate its many diverse ethnic and cultural traditions and expressions of Islam into an indigenized monolithic form is further interpreted as reticence to 'integrate'. Far too often British Muslims act in response to specific events and occurrences, very rarely taking the initiative by setting the agenda in terms of their 'Britishness'. Instead it is left to others to gauge and interpret how 'loyal' or to what extent Muslims 'belong' in Britain. To address these issues the seminar approached the notions of loyalty and belonging from two perspectives; the traditional Islamic view from the *Sharī'ah* and a contemporary perspective bearing in mind the sociological, political and legal dimensions of the discussion. Seminar papers were delivered by Imtiaz Ahmad Hussain, T J Winter, Neil Jameson, Professor Muhammad Anwar, Maleiha Malik and Dr. Bobby Sayyid. The chapters included in this publication represent the seminar papers delivered by the various contributors. Naturally, in the conversion of seminar papers and presentations into written text for publication, some editorial discretion is required, but wherever possible we have tried to remain true to the original form. This publication also includes a summary of the participants' responses. Any mistakes or shortcomings in the process of transforming the presentations into publishable papers are solely ours and not those of contributors or participants. Naturally the presenters are responsible for their views and opinions. The editors would like to express their gratitude to all the contributors and participants of the seminar and we hope that this publication will be a positive contribution to the on-going debates on citizenship, identity and belonging. We would also like to express our gratitude to Nasir Cadir for his patience and tireless efforts in the design and typesetting of this publication. In addition, we are grateful to David Middleton for his help in proof-reading the text. Finally, we thank God for His immeasurable blessings and seek His forgiveness.

The Editors

15 March 2003

Introduction

The Islamic Foundation is pleased to produce these seminar proceedings. Our staff who work in research on Muslims in Europe and Britain were very keen to hold this seminar. The Citizen Organising Foundation, a pioneering institution in its efforts in bringing together people from diverse backgrounds to work at the level of civil society for constructive social change, is an ideal partner for such an initiative.

Here in Britain there has been a recent marked increase in anti-Muslim sentiment or 'Islamophobia', which has resulted in a rise in verbal abuse and personal attacks on Muslims, their property and their mosques. The reasons for the alarming increase in these racist and anti-Muslim sentiments can be linked to events such as the *Satanic Verses* Affair, the Gulf War, the summer race riots in 2001 in the north of England and the horrific terrorist attacks on the US in September 2001. With the Muslim community unprotected due to the absence of a coherent set of laws on religious discrimination, the media have continued to provide fuel for racist fears of being overrun by Muslim asylum seekers and refugees. They have also irresponsibly presented many British Muslims as a sort of 'fifth column'. As a result, British Muslims are under scrutiny in expressed terms of their allegiances.

The changing European political climate also affects the way Muslim communities are viewed. The rise of nationalism in

Eastern Europe gave rise to a new genocide where Muslims in Bosnia and Albania have been systematically slaughtered in a savage and brutal exercise in 'ethnic cleansing'. Fascism has found favour in France, Jean-Marie Le Pen gained over 17 per cent of the votes in his presidential campaign in 2002. This translates into six million actual votes. This gives hopes to Britain's neo-Nazis in the guise of the National Front and the British National Party who gained three seats in the Burnley 2002 local elections. The assassination of Pimm Fortuyn, the Dutch politician, further polarised anti-Muslim feeling in Holland and beyond. This increase in xenophobia perpetuates the view that Muslims are 'other' and therefore do not belong here. All of these events belie the fact that a recent MORI poll (November 2001) found that 87 per cent of British Muslims declared that they are, 'loyal to Britain'. It is clear that the majority of Muslims in Britain feel comfortable being British and see no contradiction in being both Muslim and British.

When British Muslims disagree with their government on issues of political, moral or religious values as with the *Satanic Verses* Affair, the Gulf War or the bombing and invasion of Afghanistan, their contentions should not be viewed in terms of their specific loyalties or belonging to Britain. Rather, their alternative views should be interpreted as an expression of their democratic right to oppose government policies.

There is a need for British Muslims to define themselves in respect of their national and political loyalties and belonging with an emphasis on the mutualities and commonalties with the wider non-Muslim society. It is for this reason that Muslims should try to reach a broad consensus on issues pertinent to their beliefs and values that will affect them as citizens and nationals of Britain. The engagement, therefore, of Muslim scholars, from traditional religious and modern sociological disciplines, to formulate opinions and ideas in respect of full participation as a significant religious minority here in Britain is a must.

It is not an easy task to bring together the specific different views and opinions of all the religious expressions of British Muslims. However, this should not deter or inhibit the process of trying to reach agreement and formulating proactive policies and recommendations that affect all Muslims regarding their inclusion and exclusion into the wider British society.

It is to address these issues that the Islamic Foundation and the Citizen Organising Foundation organised this one-day seminar entitled, *British Muslims: Loyalty and Belonging*. We hope that by initiating the debate through this seminar that at least some important aspects of British Muslim participation and representation can be discussed. The seminar approached the issues of loyalty and belonging from two perspectives: the traditional Islamic view from the *Sharī'ah* and contemporary (sociological, political and legal) views. Both perspectives tried to analyse the challenges and obstacles that may be present. We are grateful to all of the scholars who offered their valuable time and learned opinions by way of seminar papers to these discussions. We also extend our gratitude to all of the participants who committed themselves to the seminar.

I ask Allah (SWT) to bless this sincere endeavour and trust that these proceedings will be of valuable service to the needs of British Muslims and non-Muslims alike.

Dr Manazir Ahsan
Director General, The Islamic Foundation

Message from The Home Secretary, Rt Hon David Blunkett

(Sent on 8th May 2002)

Your seminar today is an important event, not only for Britain's Muslim community, but for all those committed to the building of a safe and just society. The aims of the seminar are ones that I welcome as they will help us all to celebrate the values and benefits of diversity whilst also developing a greater sense of community responsibility, common citizenship and shared values. I have a clear vision of multi-cultural Britain – one which values the contribution made by each of our ethnic, cultural and faith communities.

The starting point is that we must treat all of our citizens equally. However it is also very important that we build on this foundation of equality to value diversity – recognising the differences in all of us and appreciating that they are a source of opportunity and strength, not a threat which should keep us apart.

Today the diverse cultural heritage of many British Muslims provides our society with an important range of unique experiences. The Government's relations with the Muslim community are and will remain extremely important. I hope that British Muslims will always find in the Government not just a sympathetic ear but a friend willing to do all it can to make this country a safe and fulfilling place to live.

I wish you all a very successful day.

Session One: **Islamic Perspectives on Loyalty and Belonging**

Muslim Loyalty and Belonging: Some Reflections on the Psychosocial Background

TIM WINTER

Our silence in the face of evil differs from that of secular people. For traditional theists, the sense of loss which evil conveys, of the fearful presence of a void, comes with a personal face: that of the devil. But the devil, being, in the Qur'ān's language, weak at plotting, carries in himself the seeds of his own downfall. The very fact that we can name him is consoling, since understanding is itself a consolation. The cruellest aspect of secularity is that its refusal to name the devil elevates him to something more than a mere personalised absence. The solace of religion, no less consoling for being painful, is that it insists that when we find no words to communicate our sense that evil has come and triumphed, our silence is one of bewilderment, not despair; of hope, not of finality.

The world is at present in the grip of fear. We fear an unknown absence that hides behind the mundanity of our experience; perhaps ubiquitous and confident, perhaps broken and at an end. Symbols of human communication such as the internet and the airlines have suddenly acquired a double meaning as the scene for a radical failure of communication. Above all, the fear is that of the unprecedented, as the world enters an age, drastically unlike its predecessors, in which religions are fragmenting into countless islands of opinion at a time when their members - and the world - are most insistently in need of their serene and consistent guidance.

At a time such as the present, a *furqān*, discernment, between true and false religion breaks surface. Despite the endless, often superbly fruitful, differences between the great world religions, the pressure of secularity has threatened each religion with a comparable confiscation of timeless certainties, and their replacement by the single certainty of change. Many now feel that they are not living in a culture, but in a kind of process, as abiding canons of beauty are replaced with styles and idioms the only expectation we can have of which is that they will briefly gratify our own sense of stylishness, then to be replaced by something no less brilliantly shallow. Post modernity, anticipated here by Andy Warhol, is occasionalistic, a series of ruptured images, hostile to nothing but the claim that we have inherited the past and that language is truly meaningful.

In such conditions, the timeless certainties of religious faith must work hard to preserve not only their consistent sense of self, but the very vocabularies with which they express their claims. The American philosopher Richard Rorty offers this account of the secularisation process:

> Europe did not *decide* to accept the idiom of Romantic poetry, or of socialist politics, or of Galilean mechanics. That sort of shift was no more an act of will than it was a result of argument. Rather, Europe gradually lost the habit of using certain words and gradually acquired the habit of using certain others.[1]

What has happened over the past century, in a steadily accelerating fashion, is that the series of mutations in values, often grounded in popular perceptions of scientific paradigm shifts, has placed the traditional vocabularies of religion under unprecedented stress. Against this background, we can see three large possibilities amidst the diversity of world faiths. Firstly, the 'time-capsule' option often embedded in local ethnic particularities, which seeks to preserve the lexicon of faith from any redefinition which might subvert the tradition's essence. The risk of anachronism or irrelevance is seen as worth running in order to preserve ancient verities for later generations that might, in some hoped-for time of penitence, return to them. Secondly, there are movements, usually called 'liberal', which adopt the secular world's reductionist vocabulary for the understanding of religion, whether this be psychological, philosophical, or sociological, and try to show how faith, or part of it, might be recoverable even if we use these terms. In the Christian context this is an established move, and has become secure enough to be popularised by such writers as John Robinson and Don Cupitt. In Islam, the marginality of Muhammad Shahrur and Farid Esack shows that for the present a thoroughgoing theological liberalism remains an elite option, despite the *de facto* popularity of attenuated and sentimental forms of 'Muslimness'.

The third possibility is to redefine the language of religion to allow it to support identity politics. Religion has, of course, always had the marking of collective and individual identity as one of its functions. However, in reaction against the threat of late modernity and post modernity to identity, and in tacit acknowledgement of the associated problematising of metaphysics and morality, this dimension has, in all the world religions, been allowed to expand beyond its natural scope and limits. Increasingly, religionists seem to define themselves sociologically, rather than theologically. The Durkheimian maxim that 'the idea of society is the soul of religion'[2] is not so far from the preoccupations of activists who are more eager to establish institutes for Islamic social sciences than to build seminaries.

The result has often been a magnification of traditional polarities between the self and the other, enabled by the steady draining-away of religiously-inspired assumptions concerning the universality of notions of honour and decency. Examples are many and diverse. Who could have thought that Buddhism, apparently the most pacific of religions, could have provided space for a movement such as Aum Shinrikyo, thousands of whose acolytes have been interrogated in connection with terrorist outrages against innocent civilians? Central to the cult's appeal, it seems, has been a redefinition of Buddhism as a movement for the preservation of East Asian identity.[3]

In India, a vegetarian creed such as Hinduism, in Gandhi's province of Gujarat, has now generated religious identity movements which, to the horror of more traditional practitioners, appear to recommend the expulsion, forced conversion, or massacre, of non-Hindu minorities. The process of the 'saffronising' of India, descending on the Ayodhya flashpoint, is seemingly well-advanced, and the prospects for regional peace and conviviality have seldom seemed less hopeful.[4]

In the universe of Islam, the same transposition of the vocabulary of faith into the vocabulary of identity is well underway. What would Averroes have made of the common modern practice of defining *Hajj* as the 'annual conference of Muslims'? Why do social scientists increasingly interpret the phenomenon of veiling in terms of the affirmation of identity? Why does congregational prayer sometimes savour of the political gesture to what is *behind* the worshippers, rather than to what lies beyond the *qiblah* wall?

The instrumentality of religion has changed, in important segments of the world faiths. God is not denied by the sloganeers of identity; rather He is enlisted as a party member. No such revivalist can entertain the suggestion that the new liberation being recommended is a group liberation *in* the world that marginalises the more fundamental project of an individual liberation *from* the world; but his vocabulary nonetheless steadily betrays him. In the Qur'ān, the word *īmān* (usually translated as 'faith') appears twenty times as frequently as the word *islām*. In the sermons of the identity merchants, the ratio usually seems to be reversed.

Neither does the instrumentality of identity advocate a return to the indigenous and the particular. Were it to do so, it would necessarily require a respectful engagement with the art, spirituality, and intellectuality of the religion's cultural provinces. And it is a shared feature of all identity politicking in world religions today that, whereas religious revivals in the great ages of faith invariably generated artistic and literary florescence, the revivalists seem to produce only impoverishment. Beauty must wait; because *da'wah*, the Mission, is more urgent; an odd logic to premodern believers, who assumed that every summons to the Real must be beautiful, and that nothing transforms a society or an individual soul more deeply than a great work of art, a building, a poem, or the serenity of a saint.

Perhaps we could even invoke this as the nearest approximation we will find to an objective yardstick against which to judge the spiritual authenticity (*aṣālah rūḥiyyah*) of religious revivals. Truth, as Plato taught, ineluctably produces beauty. The illuminated soul shines, and cannot confine the light within its own self. Whatever is done, or made, or said, or written, by such a soul, is great art, and this is part of our 'caliphal' participation and responsibility in creation. As 'Abd al-Raḥmān Jāmī puts it:

> Every beauty and perfection manifested in the theatre of the diverse grades of beings is a ray of His perfect beauty reflected therein. It is from these rays that exalted souls have received their impress of beauty and their quality of perfection.[5]

If we apply this measure, how much authenticity may we really attribute to the *soi-disant* Islamic revivalism of today?

'Say: who has forbidden the adornment of Allah which He hath brought forth for His bondmen?' (7:32). Who indeed?

The modern Muslim instrumentality of identity, then, does not seem to be about the affirmation of a culturally embedded self. The young radical activist does not really want to be a Pakistani, or an Algerian, or an American. Such a person requires what one might call a negative identity. He or she desperately desires *not* to be someone. The medievals knew God by listing all the things that God could not be; this is the strategy known as negative theology, richly deployed in both Muslim and Christian metaphysics. The moderns, it seems, being more interested in religion than in God, define religion by listing all the things that *it* cannot be. Hence Islam, we are loudly told, is a list of prohibitions. Everywhere we turn there is something we must not believe, and certainly must not do. The list of ideas entailing *shirk* (polytheism) or *bid'ah* (innovation) grows ever-longer; and no-one any longer takes pleasure and joy even in the diminishing list of things which are still allowed.

Islam, then, is about *not* being and doing things. What is left is one's identity. Because the list of prohibitions is so desperately extended, and embraces most, if not all, of the beloved practices of the village or the urban district, one is no longer allowably Sylheti, or Sarajevin. This is a questing for identity that denies real, embedded identity. As such, it often betrays its twentieth-century tributaries:

> The type and forms of cultural valuations employed by the new fundamentalist movements cannot be explained by an analysis of the tradition of Islamic religion and history; it has to be seen as an effect of inter-cultural exchange, which is fundamentally based on a Western understanding of Islam as the culture of the Other.[6]

Other, more psychological tributaries might also be cited. The shift to a culturally disembedded radicalism is often malignantly driven by a desire to wreak revenge on one's traditionalist parents or one's community for frustrations suffered at their hands. Often, too, it is perversely responsive to a global discourse that may *despise* those countries or their ethnicities. It is, in short, a way of legitimising self-hatred; a religio-legal justification of an inferiority complex. In all these cases, the radicalism shows itself responsive to Occidental influence. As John Gray puts it: 'The ideologues of political Islam are western voices, no less than Marx or Hayek. The struggle with radical Islam is yet another western family quarrel'.[7]

What, then, remains? Once the son of Pakistani migrants has stripped himself of his *shalwār*, his *pīr*, his *qawwālīs*, his *gulab jamon*, his entire sense of living as the product of a great civilisation that produced the Taj Mahal and the *ghazals* of Ghālib, what does he have left? Again, the negative theology option will define his identity as what-is-left-over; a religion of the gaps, a kind of void. That void he understands as the *Sunnah*. The *Sunnah*, that is, as figured negatively, as a list of denials, of wrenchings from disturbing memories, as a justification for the abandonment of techniques of spirituality that obstruct rather than gratify the ego.

Is this, then, a failure of religion? Is the young zealot so overwhelmed by his alienation, his humiliation, and sense of rootlessness, that the *Sunnah* which is what-is-left-over cannot restore his spirit? Surely the scriptures insist that a turn to the *Sunnah* must heal him, and help him to come to *terms* with his history and the trials of his life?

Actions, however, are by intentions. According to tradition, people tend to have the rulers they deserve, and the forces that rule the human soul are also in every case the appropriate ones for that person. The *Sunnah* is a model of sacred humanity. That is to say, humanity bathed in *sakīnah*, the peaceable 'habitation' of God's presence. 'He is the One Who sent down the *sakīnah* upon the believers' hearts, that they might grow in faith.' (48:4) This is in Sūrah al-Fatḥ, which unveils to the believing community the nature of the test that they have just passed through, and which endured for several long years. The triumph at Makkah came about not through anger, anxiety, fear, and rage at the difficult, sometimes desperate situation of the Muslims, a small island of monotheists in a pagan sea. It came about through their serenity, their *sakīnah*, which, Ibn Juzayy tells us, means stillness (*sukūn*), contentment (*ṭuma'nīnah*), and also mercy (*raḥmah*).[8] These are the gifts of reliance on Allah's promise amidst apparent misfortune. The alternative is to be of those who are described as *aẓ-ẓānnīna bi'llāhi ẓanna's-saw'*: 'Those who think ill thoughts of Allah', which, the commentators explain, means the suspicion that God will let the believers down.

The monotheistic God, of course, does *not* let the believers down. 'Weaken not; nor grieve. You are the uppermost, if you have *īmān*' (3:139): the verse revealed in the aftermath of the shock of Uhud.

So the young zealot, driven half out of his mind by his sense of alienation and despair, reads the *Sunnah* with the wrong dictionary. His view of the history of his community is one of *khidhlan* - that God has effectively abandoned it. Only a tiny, almost infinitesimal fraction of the scholars of historic Islam were even believers. The Ottoman, the Mogul, the Uzbek Khanates, the Seljuk, the Malay states, the Hausa Princedoms – all of these were lands of pure *shirk* and innovation; deserts with no oases of faith. And this conviction has to make him one of *aẓ-ẓānnīna bi'llāhi ẓanna's-saw'* - those who think ill thoughts of Allah. Their contention is that Islamic civilisation has been an atrocious, monumental, desperate failure; and the consequences of this conviction, for their religious faith, and for their ability to feel *sakīnah*, are no less disastrous. A God that has allowed the final religion to go astray so calamitously cannot, ultimately, be trusted. His policy seems usually to have been one of *khidhlān*, of the betrayal of the believers. Religion itself becomes, in Durkheim's language, entirely 'piacular', it is an attempt at cathartic, ritualised breast-beating, a rite of atonement and mourning, that seeks to channel one's fear of the uncontrollable and apparently blind forces which punish and threaten one's tribe. A cathartic component of religion has here become co-extensive with faith itself.

What it feels like to worship such a God is hard to imagine. But today, in Islam, as at the fringes of other religions, there are indeed people who worship such a deity. No peace can come of such worship, only a growing sense of being trapped inside a logic that leads only to fear and despair, unrelieved by anything more than the faintest glimmer of hope. Perhaps, the activist feels, worshipping his God, 'if we are pure enough, and angry enough, God will relent towards us; and we can anticipate the Second Coming by defying time itself, and creating a utopia for the pure somewhere on this earth'. The piacular thus accumulates into an apocalypse.

Long ago, Toynbee saw that such projects invariably end in misery. In the end, even Herod serves the oppressed community better than does Judas Maccabeus. Toynbee wrote of

'Zealotism': a psychological state - as unmistakeably pathological as it is unmistakeably exaggerated - which is one of the two possible alternative reactions of the passive party in a collision between two civilisations.[9]

The zealot, Toynbee's 'barbarian saviour-archaist', cannot imagine that faith might require the wisdom to recognise the capacities of individual human beings in different ages. Invoking a ferocious definition of *amr bi'l-ma'rūf*, 'Commanding the Good', at a time when most people are weak and struggle even to honour the basic demands of religion, betrays an abject and disastrous lack of common sense. 'Forcing religion down people's throats' will induce many of them to vomit it up again; such is the resilience or perversity of human nature. States which impose severe moral codes in public will find that they cannot deal with the proliferation of private vice, which almost masquerades as virtue in a political context where religion has identified itself with a piacular rite of repression. States which behave in such a way as to be excluded from global trade will languish in poverty, fostering disenchantment and exporting streams of refugees.

The *Sunnah*, brandished as a weapon of revenge against the sources of one's humiliation, will not allow itself to be used in this way. The *Sunnah*, as pure form, as a structure of life, cannot be itself if the inward reality of *sakīnah* is absent. The law is merciful when interpreted and applied by those who believe that God's practice towards His people has been merciful. In the hands of the zealot, it may become the most persuasive of all arguments against religion.

Actions, then, are by intentions, and the interpretation of scripture is the proof of this. Scripture is a holy place; and we need to calm ourselves before entering it. If we march in, hearts blazing with fury, viewing the world with suspicion about the divine intention, then we violate that holy place. In earlier times, only the pure of heart, and those with decades of humbling scholarship behind them, were allowed to cross the threshold into that space. Now the doors have been kicked open, and a crowd of furious, hungry, desperate men, stands quarrelling around the text.

I would like to move on now. Much of what I have said has been dismal; but religion is surely about facing reality. Too many of us today live amid delusions, no doubt because we find the reality of our times too disturbing to contemplate. Conspiracy theories, paranoia, fantasies about the past or the future; these abound in religious conferences; not just among Muslims, but among religionists everywhere. Religion, however, invites us to 'get real' - to use a very Muslim Americanism. Because we believe in God and an afterlife, and in the ultimate restitution for injustice, we should have souls great enough to look reality in the face without flinching.

My experience of the world of faith which we all inherit is, despite all that I have said about the sickness of identity mania, a positive one. I mentioned at the beginning of this lecture that there are three religious paths commonly taken today: the time-capsule, the liberal, and that of identity politics dressed up as scripturalism. The liberal option, despite the shallow purchase of its theology, is in practice widely followed among Muslims: these are the millions of individuals who may cherish the memory of a pious aunt, or perhaps a moment of religious insight earlier in their lives, or some vague sense of belonging to an inherited religious culture, but who seldom attend the mosque.

For most religiously-active Muslims, the conservative option, with a variety of variations, is the most commonly pursued. Almost all senior ulema in Sunni countries adhere to some form of conservatism, entailing adherence to one of the four Sunni *madhāhib* and to either the Ash'arī or the Māturīdī theology. Often, too, they will be actively involved in Sufism. This is a reality of which the West is largely unaware, given that it constructs its images of Muslim action from media images which inevitably focus on the frantic and the dangerous. Blaming the West for this is not entirely fair; the news media cannot be expected to focus on the pacific or the spiritual. Perhaps we need to be more frank in blaming our own Muslim communities for failing to engage in more successful and sophisticated public relations. My own encounters with television and newspaper journalists have confirmed that the mass media are only too happy to take articles from Muslims, or broadcast films made by Muslims, but that they cannot see where to find the contributions. In the United Kingdom, there is only one Muslim film production company, but several hundred cable and satellite TV channels. Major mosques and organisations have little or no public relations expertise. To accuse the West of misrepresentation is sometimes proper, but all too often reflects a hermeneutic of suspicion rooted in zealot attitudes to the Other.

What is needed, then, is for mainstream Islam to reassert its possession of *tafsīr* (exegesis). It remains in a strong position to do this. The zealots are everywhere a very small percentage of the total of believers. The masses are either too traditional or too religiously weak to want to follow them. Never will extremism triumph for long, simply because normal people do not want it. Already we find a growing sense around the Muslim world that zealotry damages only Islam, and serves its rivals. 'That which does not kill me makes me stronger', said Nietszche.

A further reason why extremism has an uncertain future is that human beings are naturally religious. Secularisation theories are now everywhere in confusion, and religion prospers mightily in most countries of the world. Belief in the transcendent is, it seems, hard-wired into our species, and what most human beings crave is not a megaphone for their frustrations, but a source of peace and serenity in a stressful world. Any religion that fails to supply that will soon be replaced by something else. There has never been an exception to this in human history. Christianity succeeded because pagan Roman religion failed to provide a sense of spiritual upliftment. Islam succeeded because the Eastern Churches were spiritually debilitated by centuries of bitter polemic. New religious movements in the West succeed by offering techniques of meditation and alternative therapies which seem absent from established religions as they are presently formulated. Islam, wherever it degenerates into a primal scream of panic about one's situation in the world, will certainly be replaced by any other religion that offers *sakīnah*.

The mainstream, then, must reclaim the initiative, and expel the zealots from the sacred place. It should not find it difficult to do this. It has, after all, a great civilisation behind it, which extremism cannot claim. It has, too, a rich tradition of spirituality, still vibrant in many countries, which, where made available to Westerners, can seem hard to resist. This was recently made plain to me by the director of the Swedish Islamic Academy. He told me that consistently, during his quarter-century as a Muslim in Stockholm, whenever he mentions that he is a Sufi, people lean forward to learn more. When he mentions Islam, they lean back, alarmed. Is this merely the expression of prejudice? Perhaps. But Muslims should also consider the possibility that Western people may be sincerely, rather than cynically, horrified by expressions of Islamic identity politics; and may be sincerely, rather than superficially, impressed by the literature and practice of traditional spiritual Islam. No-one who wishes to practice *da'wah* (invitation) in the West, or among Westernised Muslims, can afford to bypass that reality.

Once the *sakīnah* (tranquillity) has been found again, once religion becomes a matter of love of God rather than the hatred of our political and social situation, we can begin to extract our communities from the hole which we have dug for ourselves. Let us take, as a topical example, the question of suicide bombing. Historians might well wonder how this form of warfare could take root in any of the Abrahamic religions. One thinks of the kamikaze pilots of Shinto Japan, whose religious rituals, coupled with a final message read before a camera, provoked such horror and alienation in 1940s America. One thinks, too, of the self-immolation of Buddhist monks during the Vietnam War. The religious motivation behind many Tamil terrorists, rooted in a Buddhist South Asian culture, also springs to mind. Such a mentality is possible only for those who do not fully believe in a personal God, and hence have no notion of the human body as made, in some sense in God's image. For Sunni Islam, however, such a practice is historically without precedent. Coupled with the policy of targeting enemy civilians virtually at random, it is clearly the symptom of a deep-rooted sickness. It recalls the collectivist ethos (*'aṣabiyyah*) of the pre-Islamic Arabs, whose code of revenge (*tha'r*) authorised the taking of any life from a rival tribe to compensate for the loss of one of one's own, a system decisively abrogated by the Qur'an: 'no soul shall bear the burden of another' (6:164). It is also, we may speculate, connected with the phenomenon of radical religion as a form of self-hatred of which I spoke earlier. The piacular believer is so alienated from his self that he can contemplate its physical destruction, thus replicating, in Toynbee's words, 'the melodramatic suicide of the Zealots who faced hopeless military odds'.[10]

This desperation is unworthy of the *ummah* of Islam. Entirely traditional scholars speak out against it in the strongest terms, as a *bid'ah* in the most necessary sense of the term. But we need also to re-engage with the principle of *raḥmah*, of mercy, which flows from *sakīnah*. Why exactly do the *ḥadīth* suggest that Muslims must not 'destroy anyone with fire'?[11] Why are believers commanded so strongly to avoid taking the lives of civilians? One reason is because if we do this, we damage the lives of others whom we will probably never even meet. 'Whosoever kills a human being for other than murder or corruption in the earth, it will be as if he had killed all mankind' (5:32). Many suffer when one is killed. Orphans, widows, relations, friends, neighbours; all these are the victims of the single crime. Crime is never against an individual; it never has a single victim. War in the valid *Sharī'ah* sense targets only combatants, whose relatives recognise that such was their status. The targeting of civilians, however, is part of the barbarism of modern Western, Clausewitzian conflict, inflicting a deeper sense of loss and alienation; and it is entirely foreign to our heritage.

During the Second World War, my grandfather worked as a fire fighter in the London Blitz. After the war, his behaviour grew erratic, and his marriage ended painfully, inflicting shockwaves on children and a wider world of relatives. Years afterwards the reason for it all became clear. One night, after an air-raid, he had pulled from the rubble of a building the body of a small girl who looked exactly like his own daughter. The trauma of that moment never left him until he died, fifty years later. That trauma lives on, subtly, in the lives of all his descendants.

Those who take the lives of women and children, indiscriminately, and simply because they live on the other side of a frontier, should remember that they are inflicting wounds on other lives as well that can never properly be healed.

What is required, then, is an act of repentance, *tawbah*. Our communities need to turn away from the utilitarian ethic that justifies even the worst and most inhumane barbarities as expedient means, and turn back to the authentic religious teaching that it is better to suffer in patience than to descend into a tit-for-tat moral relativism that recalls the worst practices of the *Jāhiliyyah*. Religious patience, moreover, never runs out, because it knows that it will one day be crowned with glory. 'True patience', the Muslim proverb runs, 'is never exhausted.' And in the Qur'ān: 'the patient shall be given their full reward without reckoning' (39:10). The phrasing is superb. *Yuwaffā* suggests that they will be given a full, fair, proportionate reckoning; and then the phrase *bi-ghayri ḥisāb* is to be without any reckoning at all. Patience, one of the supreme Qur'ānic virtues, which led to the success of the peaceful entry into Makkah, is rewarded also in the next life, infinitely.

Here, then, is another possible yardstick against which to measure the authenticity of our Islam. Impatience *is* impiety; it is the way of the *ẓānnīna bi'llāhi ẓanna's-saw'*. And those who cannot restrain themselves will be smacked down. Worse, they will bring misfortunes upon their communities. 'Beware of a tribulation which will certainly not afflict only the wrongdoers amongst you' the Qur'ān warns us (8:25). To act impatiently on the grounds of *'aṣabiyyah*, and to defy fundamental religious teachings about the sanctity of life, and to harbour ill thoughts about God's providence - all these sins must lead, in the traditional Muslim understanding, to divine punishment. Those who regard them as a shortcut to a world in which their self-image will be healed are likely to be disappointed.

That disappointment is now palpable in the world of Islamic identity-politics. It is time that the great majority stopped being a silent majority, and raised its voice courageously. The *Sunnah* must be reclaimed as a *via positiva*.

This is not, I believe, a heroic option; it is a fundamental religious duty. To uphold the honour of Islam, as a great world religion, and to defy the voices that would turn it into little more than a resentful sect, is a *farḍ 'ayn* - an individual obligation.

We need institutions and faces that can believably do this. A few of our mosques and Islamic centres are in the grip of a small minority of worshippers who care nothing for peaceful coexistence with their fellow citizens, and whose hearts and minds are overseas. Most Muslims here, however, wish to be accepted as full and respected partners in the project of building a just and prosperous society, and do not wish their places of worship to be directed by the representatives of other governments or zealot political movements. Neither are they at ease with the reinvention of religion as a ritual of distress. This majority must now speak out. Sullenness, jealousy, lack of *tawakkul* (reliance), lack of optimism, all these are vices which must be transcended. And that transcending can only take place where religion is once again centred on the love and fear of God, not on attempts to heal a wounded pride.

I am very optimistic that this will take place. As I have already indicated, the extremists remain numerically and intellectually on the extremes. Islam is, despite the headlines, a success story. Most Muslims prefer the spiritual to the frantic; patience to the primal scream. We must now make it clear to our institutions of learning, and to those who would help us from abroad, that the principle of *shūrā* demands that the extremes be excluded, and that the voice of majoritarian Islam be allowed its natural place.

This optimism must, however, be tempered with an awareness of the immediate tactical situation. Despite the alarmism of a few intransigent voices such as Daniel Pipes and Lamin Sanneh[12] few, if any of us, respect the Middle Eastern mass-murderers who are currently inviting the world to regard Islam as the great political and moral failure of the new century. Nonetheless, we breathe the air that they have poisoned. And the poison exists here, as elsewhere, because of the aggression of a small minority of zealots.

Again, it is time to speak out in favour of normalcy. The message is a positive one: Islam is not intrinsically committed to violent reaction against the global consensus. Most scholars do not teach that globalisation obliges us to make *hijrah* to a neighbouring planet. Of course we have our own distinctive assurances on moral matters, and a deep scepticism about the ability of a consumer society to increase human fulfilment and to protect the integrity of creation. But Muslims are not committed to jumping ship. In British India, a political context far less egalitarian than the one we inhabit here, there were a few who chose the option of *hijrah* to Afghanistan. The ulema overwhelmingly stayed in place, and were not prominent during the Mutiny. 'Some scholars', as a historian of the period notes, 'held that a country remained *dāru'l-Islām* as long as a single provision of the Law was kept in force'.[13] Once the bitterness of the Mutiny had subsided, the Muslims were a peaceful presence who contributed much to the flawed but stable global enterprise that was the British Empire. Those Pathans who fought and died at Monte Cassino, the Hausas of the Nigeria Regiment who fought with the Chindits in Burma; the Bengali Lascars who died in the Battle of the Atlantic, were not conscripts, they were volunteers. Fighting against a common totalitarian enemy they were engaged, in the broad understanding of the term, in a *jihād*. One cannot deplore too strongly the attempt by a few Muslims, such as Ataullah Kopanski, to present Nazism as a potential ally for Islam.[14] Clearly, had national socialism triumphed, its scientists would have aimed at the elimination or reduction to servile status of all the non-white races of the world, not excepting the followers of Islam. To fight for the Allies was unquestionably a *jihād*.

More recently, the struggle against communism effectively united Muslims and Christendom, a long alliance which both sides seem to have forgotten with astonishing speed and completeness.

English law, with its partial legal privileging of Anglican faith, is dimly theocratic, but does not make the totalising claims which the radicals make for their own various imams. Muslims in the United Kingdom are not being offered a choice between God's law and man's. God's law, for the mainstream *fuqahā'*, is an ideal for whose realisation we cherish an ultimate hope. But it also includes the duty to act, out of *maṣlaḥah*, within the framework of laws drafted by majoritarian non-Muslim legislatures. This is, no doubt, why the tale of the Prophet Joseph was so popular in pre-modern Muslim minority contexts. Some of the greatest Muslim poetical works written in Spain after the *reconquista* were based on the story of the monotheist prophet who accepted a senior post in a non-believing political order. The story is no less popular in the villages of Tatarstan, of Muslim Siberia, and in China.

Islam, therefore, supplies arguments for loyalty. Not because it regards the present state of affairs as ideal (a view commended by no-one) but because it recognises that it is the point from which one needs to begin working towards the ideal, an ideal which will itself be reshaped by the powerful instruments of *ijtihād*. The fundamental objects, *maqāṣid*, of the *Sharī'ah* are the right to life, mind, religion, lineage, and honour; and these are respected in the legal codes of the contemporary West. We may even venture to note that they appear to be better maintained here than in the ham-fisted attempts at creating *Sharī'ah* states that we see in several corners of the Muslim world. Muslims may be unhappy with the asylum laws here, but would one wish to claim asylum in any Muslim country that currently springs to mind? We may not approve of all the rules of evidence, but would surely hesitate to claim that a murder investigation is better pursued in, say, Iran or Saudi Arabia, than under English jurisdiction.

The radicals in our inner cities, of course, will at this point revert to their primal scream. They know full well that their movements have failed, and that despite decades of effort by them there is no *Sharī'ah* order in the world. They intuit that they are engaged in acts of collective religious suicide. Yet they protest and rail against the established political order, because for them, religion has become nothing but the piacular rite of protest. Shouting at rallies and denouncing moderates are for them the most satisfying acts of worship. Were they to be denied these practices, they would be forced back on their own spiritual resources, and they are well-aware of how much they will find there.

Loyalty, then, is to the balanced, middle way, the *wasaṭ*, which is the *Sunnah*. Islam is a wisdom tradition that has seldom if ever generated extremes that have had a permanent impact. The current wave of zealotry will, I have no doubt, pass away as rapidly as it came, perhaps after some climacteric Masada. Some souls will have been damaged by it; the name of the religion will have been damaged by it, and the historians will note, with a regretful curiosity, how Islam was, for a few years, associated with terrorism. But the extremism will disappear, because no-one who has a future really desires it.

Can we accelerate this healing process? We are, I think, obliged to try. We have the advantage of knowing how to speak, and to whom to speak. The radical has to shout for a long time before anyone outside the Muslim community pays attention to him. But the traditionally-committed Muslim who is part of society at large already possesses the network. He can claim membership of one of the world's great traditions of art and literature, one that has already attracted many cultivated people in the West. Although the central mosques in most Western capitals are controlled by Saudis with no affection for the society around them, and no ability to speak to it, Islam's non-hierarchical nature means that such people can simply be circumvented. Their cultural maladroitness will always work to the mainstream's advantage. Alternative mosques and institutions of learning need to be established as a matrix for the proclamation of authentic, mainstream, spiritual, moral Islam.

There are strong reasons why this must succeed. Firstly, because everyone who has an interest in social cohesion wants it to succeed. Secondly, because unlike the Islam of those who distrust the divine purposes in history, traditional Islam is optimistic and brings *sakīnah* to the human soul. And finally, and most momentously, because it happens to be true.

Notes

1. Richard Rorty, *Contingency, Irony and Solidarity*. (repr.) New Delhi, 1989, p.6.
2. Emile Durkheim, *The Elementary Forms of the Religious Life*. (tr. J Swain.) New York, 1915, p. 419.
3. Robert Jay Lifton, *Destroying the world to save it. Aum Shinrikyo, apocalyptic violence, and the new global terrorism*. New York, 1999.
4. Brenda Crossman, *Secularism's Last Sigh? Hindutva and the (mis)rule of law*. New Delhi and Oxford, 1999.
5. Abdulkadir Emiroglu, *Molla Cami'nin Eserleri*. Ankara, 1976, p. 70.
6. Mona Abaza and Georg Stauth, 'Occidental Reason, Orientalism, Islamic Fundamentalism: A Critique', in Martin Albrow and Elizabeth King (eds.), *Globalization, Knowledge and Society*. London etc., 1990, p. 223.
7. *The Independent*, July 28, 2002.
8. Ibn Juzayy al-Kalbī, *Tafsīr*. Beirut, 1403, p. 694.
9. Arnold Toynbee, *A Study of History*. Oxford, 1939, IV, p. 639. Cf. ibid., V, p. 331 n: 'The Jewish Zealots of that age, like the Wahhhabis at the present day, combine their puritanism with militancy'.
10. Toynbee, op. cit., VI, p. 128.
11. Rudolph Peters, *Jihad in Classical and Modern Islam: A Reader*. Princeton, 1996, p. 36.
12. Lamin Sanneh, 'Sacred and Secular in Islam', *ISIM Newsletter* 10. July, 2002, p. 6 makes the following incendiary claim about the September 11 attacks: 'The West [...] has sought comfort in the convenient thought that it is only a renegade breakaway group of Muslim fundamentalists who have struck out in violence. Most Muslims do not share that view'.
13. Barbara Metcalf, *Islamic Revival in British India: Deoband 1860-1900*. Princeton, 1982, p. 51. For the muted role of the ulema during the Mutiny, see p. 82.
14. Ataullah Kopanski, *Sabres of Two Easts: an untold history of Muslims in Eastern Europe*. Islamabad, 1995.

Migration and Settlement: A Historical Perspective of Loyalty and Belonging

The aim of this paper is to examine aspects of identity, belonging and loyalty through the process of migration and the establishment of a Muslim community within the folds of a wider community. In Islamic terminology the term for migration is *hijrah*. However, it has a wider connotation than merely an act of migration; the word *hijrah* is derived from the root word *hajara*, which portrays a sense of abandoning, forsaking and leaving something. By doubling the middle letter the word becomes *hajjara*, which conveys a sense of being forced to leave or migrate. The word *hijrah,* therefore, means a migration or an emigration. There is another important term derived from the same root and that is the word *muhājir*, literally the one who has undergone the migration. The plural of this word, *muhājirūn* has more specifically been used to refer to those companions of the Prophet who migrated from Makkah to Madinah in a journey that has become well known as the *hijrah* and which became a line of demarcation between a life of religious persecution and suffering in Makkah to a new life of religious freedom in Madinah. This event was very significant and marked the dawn of a new era of progress for the Muslim community so much so that it became the starting point for the Muslim or *Hijrī* Calendar.

The Prophet expanded this meaning to include a dissociation of oneself from something by declaring that, 'A Muslim is a person who does not harm another Muslim with his tongue or hands and the émigré (*muhājir*), is the one who leaves that which God has forbidden'.[1] From an historical perspective it is quite evident that the act of *hijrah* is not a new phenomenon. In fact, from the dawn of time man has gone through the process of *hijrah*. Adam for example went through what could be described as an expulsion or banishment from paradise. Other Prophets such as Noah and Lot went through what could be described as escapist *hijrah*, in that they escaped the pending destruction of their people for their continuous disobedience to God. Abraham spent most of his life in almost a perpetual state of *hijrah*. Moses led his people on a mass *hijrah* from Egypt to the Promised Land. The process of *hijrah* may not necessarily have religious connotations as human beings naturally make *hijrah* to seek out greener pastures or are forced out by famine, invaders or natural disasters. *Hijrah* is a natural survival instinct within human beings for overcoming difficulties and hardships, which threaten their existence.

Hijrah to Abyssinia

Although the *hijrah* to Madinah is a well-known and significant fact, nevertheless, it is a surprising actuality that the first *hijrah* by Muslims occurred eight years earlier and it was to a land on the African Continent to a country known to the Arabs as al-Habashah and which became known in Europe as Abyssinia. It was at that time the most politically sophisticated unitary kingdom in Africa. The land of Abyssinia included Nubia, present day Ethiopia, Eritrea, present day Sudan and parts of Somalia. The question may be asked here as to why the Prophet ordered some of his Companions to migrate specifically to Abyssinia? The people of Makkah had strong historical links with Abyssinia. The natural location of Makkah, lying midway on the caravan route, which united the southern part of Arabia with Syria in the north, made it one of the most prosperous towns. The south-to-north commercial route connected Makkah to Yemen and across the Red Sea to Abyssinia. It was due to this trade route that the people of Makkah were well acquainted with Abyssinia, which 'was a market for the Quraish who traded there because they found food in plenty, security and good business'.² Some of the inhabitants of Makkah also had ancestral roots in Abyssinia such as Bilāl and the mother of Usāmah ibn Zayd.

There is no doubt that the persecution of Muslims in Makkah had a bearing on this decision because by the fifth year of the Prophet's mission the ferocious oppression of Muslims had intensified and there was a need for Muslims to escape. The Quraish may have thought that by persecuting and torturing the vulnerable Muslims, especially those who were poor and helpless, would cause them to give up their faith. When they discovered that this had no effect, they intensified the torture. Some were tortured repeatedly and were publicly martyred due to the torture they suffered. Finding this suffering difficult to bear the Prophet allowed some of his followers to make *hijrah* to Abyssinia:

'If you want you may go to Abyssinia, you will find there a king under whom no one suffers wrong. It is a land of truthfulness'³

The Muslims in Makkah were not able to practice their faith openly, in fact they prayed secretly and what they really longed for was to pray in peace and freedom and to be able to learn about their religion without fear or discrimination. In Abyssinia they were able to do that. *Hijrah* to Africa was not a new phenomenon. Indeed even some of the earlier Prophets had made their *hijrah* to Africa, not least Abraham, Joseph and Jesus.

Two chapters of the Qur'ān which make a link with Abyssinia had already been revealed to the Prophet Muḥammad. The first is the eighty-fifth chapter (al-Burūj), which was revealed with regard to the 'People of the Ditch'. The background to this chapter was the story of a king of Yemen, Dhūnuwās, who targeted the Christian city of Najran and started to persecute and kill people. He had a huge trench filled with fire into which he cast the Christians of Najran. The ruler of Abyssinia dispatched an army to Yemen under a commander named Eryat. The army entered Yemen and defeated Dhūnuwās. The second revelation, also related to the first, is about the invasion of Makkah by Abrahah, an officer in Eryat's army who did not approve Eryat's leadership and challenged him to a dual. Although Abrahah defeated Eryat, he suffered a wound to his lip and gained the name Abraha al-Ashram (meaning, 'one with the cut lip'). Abrahah built a fine church in the capital of Yemen and adorned it with precious stones remaining from the palace of the Queen of Sheba. But when he noticed that his beautiful building had little attraction for the people against the simple stone Ka'bah in Makkah, he decided to lead an army headed by African elephants to destroy the Ka'bah. The Chapter of the Elephant[4] gives details of what happened to that army. The time of Abrahah's expedition is known amongst the Quraish as 'the year of the Elephant'. It is interesting to note that Abrahah met the grandfather of the Prophet, 'Abd al-Muṭṭalib. When Abrahah saw him, he was impressed for 'Abd al-Muṭṭalib was tall and handsome. 'What do you need?' he was asked by Abrahah. 'Abd al-Muṭṭalib demanded that his camels be returned to him. Abrahah replied, 'I was impressed by you when I first saw you, but now I withdraw from you after you have spoken to me. You are asking me about your two hundred camels, which have been taken from you and not the house (Ka'bah), the foundation of your religion and the religion of your forefathers, which I have come to destroy and you do not speak to me about it?' 'Abd al- Muṭṭalib said to him, 'Verily I am the lord of the camels, as for the House (Ka'bah), it has a Lord who will defend it".[5] Ultimately, Abrahah failed in his attempt to destroy the Ka'bah, described in the Qur'ān as follows:

> In the name of God the Compassionate, the Merciful
> Did you not see how your Lord dealt with the companions of the elephant?
> Did he not bring all their schemes to nothing?
> Unleashing upon them flocks of birds.
> Bombarding them with stones of hard-baked clay.
> Making them like stripped wheat stalks eaten bare.[6]

Life in Abyssinia: A case study

There were, in fact, just over a hundred Muslims who made the *hijrah* to Abyssinia and each one of them had a story to tell. One such person was Ramlah Bint Abī Sufyān whose father, Abū Sufyān, was one of the Makkan leaders. She, with her husband 'Ubaydullāh Ibn Jahsh and daughter Ḥabībah, arrived in Abyssinia to live a life of freedom to practice their faith in the land of Negus. Abū Sufyān and the other leaders in Makkah found it difficult to accept that Muslims had achieved freedom to practice their faith and that Islam had been recognised at an international level. They therefore sent messengers with presents and gifts to Negus to seek their extradition. After careful examination of the Muslims' beliefs and listening to the Qur'ān, Negus declared, 'What has been revealed to your Prophet Muḥammad and what Jesus preached came from the same source'.[7] He therefore allowed the Muslims to live freely in Abyssinia and to practise their religion.

Although Ramlah enjoyed her freedom to worship freely, unfortunately she faced another hurdle. Her husband announced his rejection of Islam and his acceptance of Christianity. Abdul Wahid Hamid states: 'She made up her mind to stay in Abyssinia until such a time as God granted her relief. She divorced her husband who lived only a short while after becoming a Christian. He had given himself over to frequenting wine merchants and consuming alcohol'.[8] It should be noted that the Prophet did not order the Muslims to leave Abyssinia in spite of this conversion to Christianity. He did not even ask them to come to his aid during the battles of Badr or Uhud, which occurred when the Muslims had made *hijrah* to Madinah. The Muslim community lived in harmony with the Christian community in Abyssinia and enjoyed total freedom to practise their faith. Indeed, it was ten years later that the Prophet Muḥammad sent a proposal of marriage to Ramlah through Negus himself.

Correspondences between Negus and the Prophet

The Prophet sent many letters to rulers and kings inviting them to Islam. The letter to Negus has a special significance in that it shows respect and honour to a ruler who is seen as a believer in God. The content of the letter is as follows;

> In the name of Allah, the Beneficent, the Merciful. From Muhammad, the Messenger of God, to Najashi Azim al-Ḥabashah, Negus the stately (great) ruler of Abyssinia. Peace upon him who follows the Guidance. As to what follows, I praise God the One beside Whom there is no deity. He is the King, the Holy, the Source of Peace, the Protector and the Guardian. I bear witness that Jesus the son of Mary is the spirit belonging to God and His Word that He cast into the chaste and venerable virgin, Mary. She thus became pregnant by means of His spirit and His inspiration with Jesus in the same manner that He created Adam with His hand.
>
> I invite you to God, the One Who has no partner. Loyalty is based on His obedience. I invite you to follow me and to have absolute certainty with what I have come with. Indeed I am the Messenger of God and I invite you and your forces towards God the Mighty and Majestic. Hence I hereby bear witness that I have communicated my message and advice. I invite you to listen and accept my advice. Peace be upon him who follows true guidance.[9]

The key features of this letter are that there is a sense of cordiality and friendship. It is interesting to note that in most other letters the Prophet sent he simply declared at the beginning that, 'There is no deity but God and that Muhammad is the Messenger of God'. However, in this letter he makes mention of the miraculous birth of Jesus. This clearly indicates the Prophet understood the religious claims of the people of Abyssinia and wanted to express to them that his mission was a continuation of the prophetic tradition, which they had inherited. Another important aspect of this letter is the use of the phrase 'Loyalty is based on His obedience'. The term *mawālāh* has a wider scope than mere loyalty. It also carries a sense of protected friendship, clientage, continuity and sovereignty. All these aspects of *mawālāh* form part of the obedience to God's commands. In response to the letter sent by the Prophet Muḥammad, Negus wrote this reply:

> *In the name of God the Compassionate, the Merciful. From Negus Ashama to Muḥammad, the Messenger of Allah. Peace be upon you, O Messenger of Allah! And mercy and blessing from Allah beside whom there is no god. I have received your letter in which you have mentioned Jesus and by the Lord of heaven and earth, Jesus is not more than what you say. We fully acknowledge that with which you have been sent to us and we have entertained your cousin and his companions. I bear witness that you are the Messenger of Allah, true and confirming (those who have gone before you); I pledge to you through your cousin and surrender myself through him to the Lord of the worlds.*[10]

Delegation to Madinah

Negus also sent a delegation to the Prophet in Madinah. This delegation consisted of seven priests and five monks. They were sent to observe the Prophet, see his qualities and to listen to him and the Qur'ān. 'When they saw him and he read the Qur'ān to them, they accepted Islam and wept and they were humble'.[11] Some exegetes point towards Chapter 5 Verse 82 of the Qur'ān being revealed on this occasion:

> *And you will surely find that, of all the people, they who say,
> "We are Christians" come closest in affection for those who
> believe. This is so because there are priests and monks among
> them and these are not given to arrogance.*

The Abyssinian model and the Muslim community in Britain.

Initially, there was a one-way relationship between Makkah and
Abyssinia. Muslims migrated to Abyssinia to escape persecution
and to freely practice their faith. The Muslims in Abyssinia
could not return home. However, when the Muslims migrated
to Madinah this relationship became two-way, in so far as there
were no restrictions on travel. Correspondences were exchanged
between the Prophet and Negus, and Negus sent a delegation to
the Prophet in Madinah. The Prophet sent a proposal of
marriage to Umm Ḥabībah through Negus. Seventeen years
after the *hijrah* to Abyssinia Negus passed away. When Negus
died the Prophet prayed the funeral prayer for him. According
to the distinguished scholar, al-Safi-ur-Rahman al-
Mubarakpuri, when it became known to the Prophet that
Negus was dead, 'The Prophet announced his death and
observed prayer in absentia for him'.[12]

The Muslim community in Britain came about as a result of
contemporary *hijrah*, which has its roots in British colonialism.
The British colonised most of the Muslim world and it was only
after the Second World War that considerable numbers of
Muslims made a reverse migration to Britain. In the main this
community migrated for reasons of employment. Any
community which has migrated tends to subscribe to the view
that there will be a nostalgic return to their homeland. This is
due mainly to historical links coupled with strong family ties.
Migrant communities usually settled in the inner cities where
the likelihood of employment was at its greatest. As a result
pockets of communities mushroomed in many inner cities.
Living in 'ghetto' communities may have been interpreted as a
conscious attempt to preserve their tradition and culture.

Whereas the Muslims in Abyssinia looked towards the Prophet for guidance and inspiration, the Muslim community in Britain had to look toward each other and their links with their country of origin for moral and spiritual guidance. This reliance extended to the importing of spiritual leadership from their rural communities. This has resulted in these communities becoming inward looking and has created a barrier between themselves and the wider society. This barrier was an additional inhibitor which added to other barriers such as language and culture.

The Muslim migrant community in Abyssinia was not inward looking for there was trust with the wider community. The Muslim community in Abyssinia was also loyal to its ruler (Negus) and recognised him as their sovereign. This is proved by the fact that the Prophet addressed him as Najāshī 'Aẓīm al-Ḥabashah, 'Negus the Stately (Great) Ruler of Abyssinia'. There was no problem for the Muslims in recognising his authority. There was also a concerted expression of loyalty by the Muslim community to the King in Abyssinia. This is confirmed by Tariq Ramadan when he states:

> The Muslims thus lived in a non-Islamic environment under the authority of a leader they respected for he was fair, trustworthy and generous. Umm Salamah, who lived in Abyssinia for several years within the small group of Muslim immigrants, explained later how they had appreciated this ruler and how they had hoped that his army, although he and his people were not Muslims, would defeat its enemies.[13]

Perhaps the Muslim community in Britain does not have a problem with expressing its loyalty to the sovereign. However, when they see far right political groups rallying around national symbols such as the flag, and these being used as instruments of racial exclusion, they find it difficult to express their loyalty and belonging within such an exclusivist concept of what it means to be British.

Religious loyalty

Loyalty and belonging in Britain has been closely linked with the sovereign and state religion. Traditionally the crown chose what was 'loyal', depending on the particular beliefs of the king or queen, and demanded their subjects also be of the same religion. They often persecuted those who were not. A prime example of this is Henry VIII (1485-1509). Amelia Edwards says of Henry's persecution of Catholics:

> *'Having declared open opposition to the Church of Rome, Henry proceeded to make the most cruel enactments against the Papists; to demolish the monasteries and convents scattered by hundreds throughout his dominions... Dreadful persecutions ensued – men were hanged, burned and beheaded for not believing as he desired, and brave old Sir Thomas More and Bishop Fisher were executed for denying his royal supremacy'* [14]

It can be seen from this that to be 'loyal' to Henry VIII one had to profess the same religion as him. If you practised any other faith you were seen to be 'disloyal'. Therefore, loyalty was linked very strongly with religious conformity. Further, towards the turn of the seventeenth century many Baptists were forced to migrate to the New World in order to escape religious persecution. One such individual was Thomas Helwys, who stated that, 'The king has no right to stand between a man and his conscience, whether he be a Jew, heretic or a Turk'.[15] Helwys was perhaps one of the first religious leaders to recognise that a person's belief was not a test of loyalty.

Conclusion

In conclusion, it can be said that loyalty was closely linked and perhaps may still be with sovereign and state religion. The Muslim community in Abyssinia had close links with the Prophet and instructions were passed on to them regarding the increasing acts of worship and religious responsibilities.

Muslims in Britain however, have no direct links with the Prophet but instead rely on imported spiritual guides to interpret religious teachings. Since many of these guides come from rural agricultural communities they may not be equipped to deal with the contemporary issues and the social environment facing the Muslim community in general and its youth in particular. The Muslim youth are further hindered by language barriers; their poor usage of their mother tongue has not facilitated direct communication between the spiritual guides or religious leaders. This language barrier also exists between parents and children. In addition, the lack of opportunities in education, employment, and racism have given rise to frustrations which have erupted into acts such as riots in some inner city Muslim communities.

British Muslims can learn important lessons from the Abyssinian model. There was good will between Muslim and non-Muslim communities. The predominant Christian community granted freedom and support to the Muslim community. The Muslims for their part recognised that this freedom in turn deserved loyalty to the ruler. The most important dynamic in this relationship was the fact that there was religious freedom. This resulted in a mutual respect which bore fruit when a two-way relationship between Abyssinia and the Muslim State in Madinah developed. In the same way, the Muslim community in Britain should be willing to take an active participatory role in both the local non-Muslim community and the wider society. Islamic values and Christian values are similar and compatible. The religion of Islam is not inward looking, rather it reaches out to people and offers valuable spiritual and moral solutions to social problems. It promotes faith, which oils the wheels of social cohesion and community unity. Muslims should, therefore, actively pursue and promote basic Islamic teachings in society. The concept of *hijrah* also inculcates a 'time and space' contextualisation of its teachings and endorses a redefinition of specific cultural practices and a new understanding of faith within contemporary settings and environments. Muslims should also endeavour to become positive role models in British society. British Muslims should draw on the experiences of the early community that made *hijrah* to Abyssinia. They should realise that their *hijrah* is a natural process, which should instil them with confidence and which will assist them in fulfilling their obligations to their Creator in this world. Finally, it is well known that the Prophet Muhammad declared that migration would not stop until the sun rises from the west (i.e. until the Last Day).

Notes

1. *Ḥadīth* narrated by Bukhārī and Muslim, in al-Nawawī, *Riyāḍ-us-Ṣāliḥīn*. New Delhi, 1989, p.147.
2. al-Ṭabarī, *Annales* (ed. M. J. de Goeje). Leiden, 1901, Vol 1, 3, p.1180.
3. Ibn Isḥāq, *Sīrah Rasūl Allāh*. p.208.
4. Qur'ān, Chapter 105.
5. Ibn Kathīr, *Tafsīr Ibn Kathīr*. Dār al-Qur'ān al-Karīm, Beirut, 7th edition, 1981, p.677.
6. Qur'ān, op. cit.
7. Ibn Hishām, *Sīrah Rasūl Allāh*. Cairo, p.152.
8. Abdul Wahid Hamid, *Companions of the Prophet*, book two. MELS, London, 1995, p.89.
9. *Zād al-Ma'ād*, in Safi ur-Rahman al-Mubarakpuri, *Ar-Raheeq al-Makhtum (The Sealed Nectar)*. Riyad, 1996.
10. *Zād al-Ma'ād*, ibid.
11. Tujibī, *Mukhtaṣar min Tafsīr al-Imām al-Ṭabarī*, 2 vols. Cairo, 1971, p.152.
12. Safi ur-Rahman al-Mubarakpuri, *Ar-Raheeq al-Makhtum (The Sealed Nectar)*. Riyad, 1996, p. 352.
13. Tariq Ramadan, *To be a European Muslim*. Leicester, 1999, p.168.
14. Amelia Edwards, *A Summary of English History*. London, 1860, p. 43.
15. Thomas Helwys, 'The Mystery of Iniquity' in David George Mullen, *Religious Pluralism in the West*. Oxford, 1998, p.134.

Discussion

(Discussions and comments in this text are not verbatim quotations, but a summary of the proceedings. The name of the participant is in capitals, while comments from speakers are in italics.)

IBRAHIM HEWITT: It was said that being British in the context of being a British Muslim was a 'double-edged sword' and that the recent interest and rise in 'regionalism' and post-colonial migration has brought into question the whole notion of what it means to be British. Whereas, traditionally, being British has been synonymous with being English, white and Christian the advent of these two social phenomena has widened interpretations of 'Britishness'.

ADIL SALAHI: (A detailed discussion on the concept of *naṣīḥah*, or 'good counsel' to the leader of society based on the *Ḥadīth* was undertaken.) Did the Muslim community give good counsel to the Prime Minister? Some participants questioned whether good counsel was due from a Muslim to a non-Muslim leader.

The speakers stressed that this notion of 'good counsel' would extend to Muslim communities living as religious minorities, ruled by non-Muslims. In the case of a conflict of interests where there might be a disagreement with government policy, there is a democratic right of dissent and in the case of armed conflict, conscientious objection. Participants also mentioned that many organisations had been in contact with Downing Street in the wake of September 11th, particularly the MCB.

YAHYA BIRT: The fact that young British Muslims are largely seen as disaffected and disengaged with the wider British society extends beyond their perceived 'foreignness' and is perhaps part of a wider phenomenon affecting all British youth, largely as a result of the increasing mass multi-media information culture. It was noted that dissent was very much a historical tradition within British society.

ZAHID PARVEZ: The 'identity crisis' experienced amongst young British Muslims of South Asian origin raises serious questions about the concept and interpretations of 'integration'. What do we mean by this term? Are we suggesting subscription to a cultural monolith at the expense of all other social sub-cultures? The social exclusion of British Muslims, young and old, has had very adverse effects on their 'loyalties' which are always viewed in absolute terms.

The historical examples given of Muslims living as minority communities do not suggest a process of ghettoisation. This is a recent phenomenon, perhaps as a means of preserving cultural identity and values. Traditionally Muslim minority communities have been largely interactive. Social integration in modern societies where the idea of community has been eroded is very problematic, particularly where institutionalised racism forms a huge stumbling block for people to get to know and understand each other.

BRUNEL JONES: Occasions of a shared sense of Britishness are witnessed through national events such as the Queen Mother's funeral, when the majority of citizens express their national pride and manifest very visibly their loyalty and belonging. This was exampled by the military pallbearers, one of whom was clearly racially different and possibly Muslim by name. It is a very British military notion of 'fighting for the Crown' and the United Kingdom is a crucible of the idea of fighting together. Would Muslims find it possible to fight for the Crown?

Muslims are well acquainted with the chivalrous principles of fighting for justice and have historically died in the service of crown and country. Examples were cited of the large numbers of Muslims who served in the navy during WWII as part of the British Armed Forces. Unfortunately, they are not celebrated or commemorated. In recent times there has been a slow uptake of Muslims into the Armed Forces; perhaps this is because of the memory of the colonial period or the fact that racism exists in the Armed Forces.

Session Two: **British Muslims – Influencing UK Public Life: A Case Study**

British Muslims – Influencing UK Public Life: A Case Study

NEIL JAMESON

> As *humanity enters the third millennium of the Christian era,*
> *waves of globalisation and floods of information are forcing*
> *human beings in almost every part of the world to become*
> *citizens of the 'global village'. A need for mutual understanding*
> *and dialogue between peoples belonging to different religions,*
> *cultures and ideologies was never as great and as pressing as it is*
> *today. It would not be going too far to suggest that this is*
> *becoming a prerequisite for the survival and sustenance of*
> *human society. No one can afford to live in isolation.*[1]

'Peace be upon you' and the response of 'Peace also be with you'
is the greeting, the challenge, the agitational question, and the
goal of all relationships in Islam. How to bring about that 'peace
in the Lord' is the ultimate quest shared by the world's great
religions. My understanding of Islam is that this peace is best
achieved through struggle or *jihād* – and that there is no short
cut way of achieving it other than through action and reflection
whilst trying to bring about a more just world.

Professor Khurshid's challenging Foreword to *Building a
New Society* by Zahid Parvez goes on to say:

'A Clash of Civilisations' is the worst scenario; co-existence, co-operation and the creation of a healthy confluence are definitely alternatives'.[2]

A year earlier, Sam Huntington published his now best seller *'The Clash of Civilisations and the Remaking of World Order'*.[3] He argues that conflicts between civilisations and religions would dominate the future stability of the world – yet an understanding of such tensions and a framework for co-existence and mutual respect was the way of peace and progress. Professor Khurshid calls for dialogue between religions, cultures and ideologies and lays the responsibility for initiating this firmly at the door of Muslims living in the West. He goes on to say:

> *Dialogue presupposes a readiness to think and talk, to discuss and even differ without conflict and confrontation. It can hardly flourish among those who choose to be deaf and dumb. For we can talk to each other with confidence only if we are clear about what we are, and what our vision of the future is.*

And yet it is not easy! We are in the middle of an identity crisis, not just in the UK but throughout the world. Many of us do not know who or what we are. Some have impossibly naive notions of what they should be; they cling to a romanticised heritage, subscribe to an unchanging tradition and are ready to kill or be killed to save some essence of a fixed identity. Others have abandoned the very idea of a fixed identity; they change their identity with as much ease as they change their designer trainers. To 'know thyself' as Socrates put it, is both a fundamental human urge and a basic question in philosophy. But in a rapidly globalising world, all those things which once provided us with a sense of confidence in ourselves – nation states with a homogeneous population, well established local communities, allegiance to history and tradition – are all being challenged. The Queen in her speech to Parliament on 31st April 2002, made reference to the massive changes that have taken place in Britain since her Coronation in 1953 – then, more or less uniform and Anglican, now multi- cultural and multi- faith.

So how do we now construct our identity? Cornel West[4] has suggested we do this from the building blocks of our desires – or by understanding our self interest:

- the human desire for recognition
- the quest for visibility
- the sense of being acknowledged
- the deep desire for association.

Barry Knight, one of COF's academic allies from the UK think tank CENTRIS has just undertaken research in 47 Commonwealth countries for the Commonwealth Foundation. Based on thousands of responses this research, concerned with the challenge of 'Reviving Democracy', concluded similar findings to West. Knight[5] states that of those surveyed from many different cultures and religions the same request came for:

- bread and water
- recognition
- freedom to associate with others.

If Cornell and Knight are right, and their conclusion echoes our own experience, then religion, and Islam in particular, in the UK of 2002 has much to offer us in our quest for identity. Certainly, at its best, it gives us recognition and provides a framework of behaviour and beliefs which help us make sense of the world and place our own struggles in some historical context. The danger is that many people cling to religion as a sort of protective clothing from the rigours of public life – becoming ever more zealous and unquestioning in the face of an increasingly complex world and sophisticated media.

But to simply use religion to gain our identity and some form of recognition is to be partial and deny the other aspects of our self interest which Knight and Cornell refer to – what Islam has to say about the struggle for bread and water and our human need, or obligation to associate with others. Parvez makes it clear that Islamic methodology prescribes that Islam must be presented and shared with the public at large (*da'wah*) and that this must be done in as peaceful and gracious a way as possible through interaction, conversation and social and political participation. Indeed, he says that Islam positively denounces monasticism and enjoins instead family, community, integration, cooperation and mutual respect. In the section of his book which offers 'A practical framework for positive change',[6] Parvez applauds the role and potential of the mosque in UK communities – particularly where it provides more than just a worship centre or focus for identity for an ethnic or geographical community. He argues that the mosque can still be the centre for community life – offering teaching, counselling, support for the vulnerable, succour for the lonely and guidance on citizenship and survival in a pluralist society.

The challenge for all the world's great religions in the face of an increasingly dominant market place, led by the global corporations of consumerism and finance, is partly to recognise this as a major threat to the core values of each religion – and partly to adjust and develop that which we do best in the face of such threats and temptations. The word 'religion' is derived from the word 'religade' which literally means to 'bind together'. How 'People of the Book' use their religion to 'do' politics and to do this non-violently and democratically is the great challenge we face today. How best should our mosques and churches prepare our people to challenge a system which creates injustice, winners and losers and an unequal distribution of resources – how to perform *jihād* today and still be effective and gracious remains a dilemma for many.

It is understandably tempting, therefore, to abdicate to the government the responsibility for meeting our human need for bread and water, to use our faith and the cultural practices which are associated with it to give us identity and recognition and to associate but only ever with people who agree with us –

or worse to nurture amongst Muslims living in the West a condition of *kufr* (or living amongst unbelievers). A powerful sense of *kufr* helps the believer to live in Western exile in a state of chronic persecution, from which a limited sort of theology is born, and on which its survival depends. There has to be a more constructive and life giving alternative for the British Muslims now determined to make their way in this country and still be loyal to the tenets of the faith and its obligation on 'believers' to change and challenge injustice wherever it is found. It is this alternative that The Citizen Organising Foundation (COF) is determined to both promote and develop. At its most basic and effective, broad based citizen or community organising is a tool or technique which religious congregations can use to meet Knight's objectives of:

- seeking 'bread and water', fairly distributed for all through collective action intended to revive UK public life and non partisan politics

- demanding 'recognition' as an organised and confidant community with a part to play and a valid contribution to make to the governance of this country

- freely and comfortably associating with others through discourse, debate, common action and shared experiences which challenge stereotypes, racism and the fear of strangers.

The COF teaches the 'art of politics' to thousands of community leaders drawn from this country's mosques, churches, schools, colleges and unions. By 'politics' we do not mean partisan or ideologically based narrow electoral politics or voting. This has its place in the running of any community but it cannot be the only option on offer. Recently, in my community of Stepney in east London, many Muslims queued up to try and be elected as a councillor in Tower Hamlets where all the main parties fielded Muslim candidates. This is obviously a healthy development and reflects a growing confidence by east

London's Muslim community in representative democracy and a local council's ability to influence public life. However, I would also like to mention an equally significant development and event which took place on 30th April 2002, a public assembly convened by one of COF's local affiliate organisations, *The East London Communities Organisation* (TELCO). Nearly 300 people from Tower Hamlets filled the entrance hall at the local college to hold an 'Accountability Assembly' with the main party leaders. TELCO's ten member communities in the Borough had spent three months in dialogue with their members and each other and built their own agenda for the Borough. On the platform the five TELCO co-chairs lined up to confront the four party leaders and try to persuade them to both recognise and endorse TELCO's broad agenda for change. Three Muslims, two young women and a male student from the college, held the platform along with a Buddhist and a union leader from the local UNISON branch. They had all rehearsed together, agreed their position, gained the consent of their member groups and were set to try and hold the more experienced party leaders to account. The hall was filled by leaders from the East London Mosque, students from Stepney Green School and Tower Hamlets College, London's Buddhist Community, two Roman Catholic congregations, three UNISON union branches and over forty Muslim women from a local Community Centre. The meeting was also supported by ten students from COF's Young Citizens alliance in the Midlands, mostly young Muslim people, with COF's Muslim Organiser, Faraz Yousufzai.

The issues that this alliance had agreed to support were not specifically Muslim issues – nor was the language that evening particularly Islamic. In a pluralist society like East London the politics COF promotes is the ancient politics of 'the common good' – the politics of compromise, dialogue and pragmatism. Since TELCO's member communities all share the same values their agenda was inevitably biased towards the vulnerable. Prospective Council Leaders were asked to back TELCO's campaign for a 'Living Wage'; to work with TELCO's 'organised young people' to reshape the youth service; to promise a programme of affordable family housing for local people in neighbourhoods which are cleaned regularly and free from crime and decay. When the sitting leader of the Labour Group, and thus leader of the Council, responded with a vague answer, the seventeen year old Muslim student in the Chair asked the Assembly to score what he had said – was it a 'Yes' or was it a 'No'? or was it a 'wishy-washy'? reply. It was voted a unanimous 'wishy-washy'! The Council leader, himself a Muslim and the first Bengali Council leader in the country, left the hall smarting a little – but hopefully still interested in working with TELCO after the election, since, after five years and many different campaigns, TELCO is now one of the power players of East London.

Another interesting feature of the local elections of 2002 was that several of those standing in local wards came to politics through their mosque or a group like the Islamic Society of Britain (ISB), or Young Muslims (YM) or Young Muslim Organisation (YMO). Some of them were trained at one of COF's intensive five day training programmes and became active in TELCO where the rule is you have to work with people who are different to you and where the responsibility of the delegate to liaise and teach back to the group from which they came is strongly emphasised. Many have called TELCO a 'University of the Streets' which is a fair description. Our aim is for the constituent bodies of TELCO to see themselves not just as worship centres, schools or union branches, but institutions with a responsibility to train and develop leaders, to teach faith and its value system in the context of east London today which means coexistence and mutual respect if tolerance is to grow and prejudice be challenged. TELCO teaches that diversity is a political strength and that people have more in common than elements which divide. We can agree that all in work should be paid a fair wage, that families should be housed properly and anti-social behaviour challenged. We cannot, however, agree on approaches to God or partisan political positions, so the best TELCO leaders avoid these issues and build relationships of mutual respect around an agenda for action we can agree on and can fight for together. These will not thus, by definition, simply be Muslim issues or Christian issues etc.

The COF's analysis of the world has changed with the world in the twelve years of our organising citizens in the UK. While the role and dominance of global companies and culture grows internationally so does the power and significance of governments, local and national.[7] The responsibility of the key institutions of family, faith and labour to hold the balance between these two power players is even more important now than ever. Our hope for the next ten years is that British Muslims and their institutions will put their time, energy and resources into building strong, non-partisan, inclusive, training organisations like TELCO that depend on strong and vibrant institutions to survive and flourish. The task of training and developing the next generation of community leaders so that they can operate inclusively, and with the skill and professionalism needed to be effective in public life, is quite a challenge. But it is a role our mosques and groups are beginning to perform with confidence and in association with the COF and groups like TELCO in East London and CITIZENS in the West Midlands.

Each time you greet or are greeted with the traditional 'Peace be upon you' remember this is not just a politeness. It is a political, agitational challenge to have a strategy, develop our people, work with others, seek recognition and challenge injustice wherever it is found – and thus bring about that 'Peace' we are born to create and sustain.

Notes

1. Zahid Parvez, *Building a New Society – An Islamic Approach to Social Change*. Revival Publications, Leicester, 2001, p. ix.

2. Parvez, ibid.
3. Samuel P. Huntington, *The Clash of Civilisations and the Remaking of World Order*. Touchstone Books, 1997.
4. See Jim Wallisetal, *The Soul of Politics: A Practical and Prophetic Vision for Change*, The New Press, 1996, 320pp.
5. Knight, Chigudu and Tandon, *Reviving Democracy – Citizens at the Heart of Governance*. Earthscan, 2002.
6. Parvez, Op. Cit, p. 229.
7. See Thomas Friedman, *The Lexus and the Olive Tree – Understanding Globalisation*. Anchor Books, 2000, and George Monbiot, *Captive State – The Corporate Takeover of Britain*. Macmillan, 2000.

Discussion

SEAN McLOUGHLIN: The problem of participation in civil society is not unique to British Muslims and, within our multicultural society other faith communities like the Christians and Jews also experience similar problems. Furthermore, throughout Europe disengagement and social exclusion by social minorities is experienced in varying degrees and this phenomenon has been studied by many scholars. What prevents people involving themselves in the political process?

NEIL JAMESON: *This is why the COF seeks to engage social minorities and faith communities in the political process. We try to help people understand politics beyond the hurly-burly of party politics and the election cross on a ballot paper and, instead, to move towards the relevance of political participation. We try to get people to realise that there is strength in unity and that political powers do not always want popular participation. People are usually busy in other, more enjoyable, endeavours. In the case of TELCO, one of our difficulties is to convince mosques of the need for political participation through this organisation and that they should pay (a thousand pounds) to be a member, of a forum such as TELCO.*

SEAMUS MARTIN: The need and existence of the COF was questioned in view of the fact that most inner-city local councils are well represented by Muslims, particularly the example cited in Tower Hamlets.

NEIL JAMESON: *The COF is pro-democratic and it seeks to raise political awareness amongst social minorities. It also recognises that local councils cannot act alone and that public political engagement at an individual level is vital for the democratic process to be effective and representative. The worry is self-exclusion via non-participation because of an increasing disenfranchment of British Muslims and the role of the COF is vital in engaging the dispossessed and encouraging Muslims to get politically involved.*

MALEIHA MALIK: Local political involvement forces more global changes and Muslims are therefore more effective at this level. For example, the European Human Rights Act should be a focus for active participation by forcing the national government to implement it.

YAHYA BIRT: With the erosion of regional power and representation of local government under the Conservatives, the question was raised of how the COF negotiated this new political environment particularly in terms of trying to empower social minorities.

NEIL JAMESON: *Whilst there has been a definite erosion of local political representation, there has been a noticeable revival in civil society and the engagement of organisations like the East London Mosque as prime examples and models of civil and social action. The 'persuasion of need' is the best way of precipitating political and social action and the COF seeks to activate a 'conversation between faiths' so that we may achieve a deeper understanding of our own faith and others in the light of increasing secularisation.*

REV. ANGUS RITCHIE: The position of faith in secular society is largely private and in the public space we all meet as consumers. The COF allows people to enter into a dialogue with others of a different tradition and culture seeking commonalities. It also puts people in touch with the realities of the struggle for justice and equality in society.

Session Three: **Facing Social, Legal and Political Realities**

British Muslims:
Socio-Economic Position

PROFESSOR MUHAMMAD ANWAR

In relation to the position of Muslims in Britain, I would firstly like to make some general points to put this paper into a wider context. Some of these points have been raised in other papers in this publication but I would like to go through them again systematically. I would then like to move on to briefly analyse the socio-economic position of Muslims, particularly looking at disadvantage and discrimination; then again briefly, within the limits of this paper, examine how far Muslims are represented on elected and appointed bodies. I would then like to look at the role of the media. Further, within this context, I will offer some comments about the National Front and the British National Party, which is alarmingly quite topical these days. Finally, looking to the future, I would like to suggest how we might deal with some of the diversity and equality issues faced by British Muslims. Obviously this paper is very selective and quite short in detail because of the confines and limits of the seminar.

The first general point is with regard to the Muslim population of Britain. Some estimates claim that there are two million whilst others say there are around 3 million Muslims in Britain. My estimates show that there are 1.8 million Muslims. Table 1 also shows figures for other religious groups in Britain.

Table 1: Religious Affiliation in Britain: Estimates for 2000

		Million
1.	Christian denominations	
	Anglicans	26.2
	Roman Catholics	5.7
	Presbyterians	2.6
	Methodists	1.3
	Black-majority Pentecostal and Holiness Churches	0.5
2.	Muslims	1.8
3.	Sikhs	0.5
4.	Hindus	0.5
5.	Jews	0.3

With regard to the populations of religious entities in Britain, there was a question in the 2001 Census about religious affiliation. It was not a compulsory question, but, instead, voluntary, and we expect a more accurate picture to emerge as the results of the latest census are made available from February 2003. Even with new technology and improved data collection methods, it is still going to take approximately three years for the detailed information from the 2001 Census to become widely available. However, it is obvious from Table 1 that Muslims are the largest religious minority group in Britain. They are highly concentrated and I think this concentration is very important in respect of the issues which were being raised through this seminar. Almost 60 per cent of Muslims live in the South-East, mainly in the Greater London area, I believe this is something which has a significant bearing on political participation, integration and other factors.

Muslims are not a homogeneous group. They come from different countries, they speak different languages, they belong to different ethnic groups, and therefore we should not expect that they should be united on everything. Their backgrounds obviously do make a difference, and the identity issue is an interesting one in this context. I think it is important to mention that they are *British* Muslims. According to the statistics, I estimate that almost 60 per cent of Muslims are actually now British-born and that there are many more who came here as children. As a result, the demographic change which is taking place is very visible and, at the same time, very important when we talk about British Muslims.

Looking to the future in terms of the number of Muslims, the projected estimates are listed below (see Table 2). These figures represent estimates of ethnic minority groups based on the Census in 1991.

Table 2: **Ethnic Minority Population: Estimates for 1998 and 2020 (Britain)**

	Population (thousands)	
Ethnic Group	1998	2020
White (other than Irish)	50986	49000
African	354	700
Afro-Caribbean	797	1000
Bangladeshi	232	460
Pakistani	567	1250
Indian	945	1200
Chinese	167	250
Various	601	1000
Irish	2092	3000
Total	56741	57860

If we examine the projections for 2020, especially for the two main Muslim groups, Bangladeshis and Pakistanis, the Bangladeshi population in 2020 is going to be roughly double the size of that in 1998 and for the Pakistanis, it is estimated to be more than double. Based on the current figures this is how I estimate what sort of demographic changes are likely to take place. We do not have information regarding other Muslim groups, but I hope we will obtain this from the 2001 Census available next year. The population of British Muslims is going to increase in the future based, as we can see, on these estimates.

I think with the generational change that has taken place we can also see the changes in attitudes as well as behaviour of young British Muslims. This is very significant in relation to the first generation migrant Muslims, and the second or third generation Muslims who were born and brought up in this country. Any changes we see in their behaviour are linked to the way in which they are being brought up in this country, and the way they feel about different issues. We should not be surprised if the views of the second and third generations are not always compatible with the views of their parents. This is a phenomenon we need to understand and accommodate.

The new generations of British Muslims expect to be treated as equal British citizens. However, all the available evidence shows that they are not being treated equally by the institutions of our society. I believe this is the main obstacle in terms of their integration into the wider British society.

It is important that Muslims in Britain are not seen in isolation although there have been events, national and international, which are specifically relevant to them. The disturbances which took place in 2001 in Burnley, Bradford and Oldham, and the tragic September 11 events in the US are relevant; as are the ongoing conflicts in Kashmir and the Middle East. For the main relevant events in relation to British Muslims that have taken place in the last few years I propose the list below (Table 3).

Table 3: **Main Events Relevant to British Muslims**

> The Rushdie Affair, 1989
> The Gulf War, 1991
> The Bosnian situation, 1990s

Urban unrest in Oldham, Burnley, Bradford, 2001
The tragic events in the US on 11th September 2001
War in Afghanistan, 2001 and 2002
The on-going conflict in Kashmir and the Middle East

It is because of these events that we cannot view British Muslims in isolation. Events that occur in other Muslim countries and beyond, or in this country for that matter involving Muslims, have direct relevance for British Muslims. Therefore we need to see them in a wider context, the global context, and not just with respect to what is happening in Britain.

Let us now examine some of the disadvantages and discrimination faced by British Muslims. In education, the general conclusion is that the academic achievement levels of Muslim children are generally lower than white and some other ethnic minority children – for example, when compared with Indian and Chinese children. But not all Muslim children are under-achieving. These are general patterns and are not about individuals. I could equally cite 10 or 20 individuals who have done very well, but these are the general patterns we are discussing. In this context, there are area differences, for example, the educational achievements of children in Birmingham and Bradford, are far lower in comparison with Muslim children from London or Glasgow. They are also generally linked to social class and the type of schools they attend. However, generally, we find that Muslim children are under-achieving. But there is also a very interesting development taking place: Muslim girls are doing better than Muslim boys. There is a national trend in this country that girls are doing better than boys, and the figures shown below from Birmingham prove this point. As mentioned, this trend is also true for Muslim children. The figures show that of Pakistani boys in the year 2000, 27 per cent achieved 5 A* to C grades compared with 41 per cent of Pakistani girls. The same pattern applies to Bangladeshi children. (see Table 4). There are similar statistics in relation to other areas also. From the figures shown, it is a myth that Muslim parents are holding their girls back from education. If we compare university statistics, they prove that Muslim girls are doing very well and that they are getting into higher education in increasing numbers. There may be isolated cases where this is not happening, but generally the trend is upward in terms of achievement.

Table 4: Trends in GCSE Performance by Ethnic Group and Gender in Birmingham – 5 A* – C GRADES

Ethnicity/Gender	1998 %	2000 %	Improvement 1998-2000 %
Afro Caribbean boys	13	19	6
Afro Caribbean girls	28	31	3
Bangladeshi boys	28	30	2
Bangladeshi girls	36	42	6
Indian boys	40	49	9
Indian girls	50	61	11
Pakistani boys	21	27	6
Pakistani girls	31	41	10
White boys	34	36	2
White girls	44	45	1
All boys	30	34	4
All girls	42	47	5

There are other education issues worthy of mention here. There is the issue of religious education, mother tongue teaching in many regions and the provision of *ḥalāl* meat, which is still an issue in some areas. But generally the authorities are responding well with provision for prayer facilities, uniforms for girls, single-sex education, and state funding of schools. My figures show that there are 85 Muslim independent schools but only 5 are state-funded.

Looking at employment, which is used as another indicator for integration, the main problem facing Muslims is the very high level of unemployment rates. Because statistics about employment do not include ethnic categories, we have to rely on other sources, like statistics from areas where Muslims are concentrated. For example, if we look at 10 inner city wards in Birmingham where most Muslims live (see Table 5) we find that they have the highest unemployment rates in the whole of Birmingham. A similar exercise could be undertaken in other areas.

Table 5: **Top 10 Wards in Birmingham with the Highest Levels of Unemployment – April 1998**

Ward	Unemployment Level %
Sparkbrook	25.3
Aston	23.4
Ladywood	21.3
Nechells	19.7
Handsworth	19.1
Sparkhill	17.1
Small Heath	16.5
Soho	16.3
Washwood Heath	14.7
Edgbaston	11.7
Birmingham Average	9.6

We also find that nationally the unemployment rate for Muslim groups, and here we are talking about mainly Pakistanis and Bangladeshis, is about 25 per cent compared with the *national* unemployment rate of 3.6 per cent. But in some areas for Muslims the unemployment rate is over 30 per cent, and this applies to both men and women.

Another point worth mentioning here is that very few Muslim women actually work: 22 per cent are economically active, and out of them only 11 per cent are employed. So if we compare this figure with that for Indian women: 54 per cent of Indian women work. In addition, about 50 per cent of white women are in employment. Therefore we can see that Muslim women are basically very low down in terms of employment.

With regards to the housing situation, there are three issues that need to be mentioned. Firstly, that the owner-occupation rate among Muslims is high compared with white people in particular, and not as high compared with Indian groups. Secondly, the condition of the houses in which Muslims live is generally bad. This is based on a survey and information from the 1991 Census. And thirdly, Muslims generally live in run-down inner-city areas and therefore face all the problems of such areas.

Evidence shows that there is now a clear shift taking place from racial discrimination to religious and cultural discrimination. There are many published reports in relation to this. Also, Muslim women in particular are not only facing religious discrimination, but also racial and gender discrimination. We have completed a research project on this, a qualitative study, which gave us a great deal of information regarding Muslim women's experiences of multi-level discrimination.[1]

Let me move on to the political participation and representation of Muslims. Most Muslims in Britain, unlike in some other West European countries, have a right to vote and stand for election. This is because they are either British citizens or Commonwealth citizens. However, there are still some Muslims who do not enjoy this right. Since Muslims are concentrated in some inner city areas, therefore, at least in theory they are in a position to influence the outcome of elections in those areas. The East End of London is a good example because Muslims there are highly concentrated, and the political parties cannot ignore this demographic reality. They are located in situations where they can statistically influence the electoral process. But when we look at what they have achieved in terms of representation, it is minimal. At the local level there is a slight improvement. We estimate that there are over two hundred Muslim councillors in Britain. But if we look at the House of Commons there are only two MPs of Muslim origin out of 659, indicating that British Muslims have a long way to go. If we look at the number of Muslims in the population we could argue that in order to reflect that in the House of Commons there should be around 20 MPs of Muslim origin. In the House of Lords there are four life peers of Muslim origin or who have Muslim names. This is perhaps because these positions are honorary and are based on appointments. There is no Muslim representation in the Scottish Parliament or in the Welsh Assembly and no-one of Muslim origin has been elected to the Greater London Assembly. In the European Parliament there is one British MEP of Muslim origin. However, at local level there are now more developments. For example, some councils have leaders, at least one, and several have deputy leaders of Muslim origin. In some cases they also chair important committees. Furthermore, there are also a few mayors of Muslim origin.

If we examine public appointments there are very few Muslims who are appointed onto public bodies. They are also under-represented in the Civil Service and in the Armed Forces. Although these numbers are increasing it is at a very slow pace. Therefore, I believe it is going to take a long time to reflect the number of Muslims in the population in these services.

Another area where Muslims lack representation is the media. The role of the media is obviously very important in our multi-religious society. I am afraid that the role of the media is generally, and historically, quite negative in relation to British Muslims. The images presented by the media often reinforce stereotyping and they contribute to what we call Islamophobia. The situation after the September 11 obviously has not helped, if anything things have got worse. The negative coverage of the disturbances in Burnley, Oldham and Bradford by the media has also damaged community relations. The extreme right groups are obviously exploiting this situation and are creating problems for British Muslims. We have seen it not only in this country, but also in other European countries. As we know, three British

Nationalist Party (BNP) candidates were elected in Burnley in the recent local elections. If one analyses the situation and scrutinises the performance of other BNP candidates, the indicators show an increased move towards the far right which represents a real danger to minorities and to community cohesion.

Muslims therefore need to be on their guard because the thrust of the far right's arguments and the negative images that are being presented are mainly targeted against Muslims. Furthermore, after the September 11 incident there is increased fear among Muslims. We have evidence of attacks and although they are not systematic, the indications are that the number of attacks against individuals and property has risen. As a result, there is a lot of anxiety among British Muslims. There have been an increasing number of cases reported, not just by people in this country but also by the European Monitoring Centre on Racism and Xenophobia (EUMC) based in Vienna. I would suggest that British Muslims' loyalty to this country is being questioned and mainly raised by the media. I think the differences of political and moral opinions expressed by British Muslims are being labelled as disloyalty. If non-Muslims, for example, say something about the war in Afghanistan it is all right, that is regarded as a difference of opinion. However, if a Muslim leader says something similar it is termed as disloyalty. So it is, in this way, that I believe Muslims are obviously being targeted. In my opinion, the media has presented the views of a tiny minority of extremist and fanatical British Muslims who have made the headlines, and this in turn has seriously damaged community relations between Muslims and others.

So where do we go from here? What sort of action is required to deal with the issues I have outlined above? Very briefly, I would like to make seven suggestions:

1   Like race and sex discrimination, religious discrimination should be made unlawful in Britain.

2   Targeted policies are needed to tackle disadvantage, poverty and deprivation among British Muslims.

3   Employers and service providers need to provide facilities for Muslims for the practice of their religion and to meet their cultural needs.

4   The media should be sensitive to the feelings of Muslims when reporting issues involving religion and religious groups.

5   All political parties should ensure that Muslims are appropriately represented at local and national levels in elected bodies and in public appointments.

6   It is important that Muslim parents and leaders play their role educating their children and members in order to help them to be good citizens.

7   There should be more dialogue between British Muslims and other communities nationally and locally to create better understanding and to unite diverse communities.

Notes

1. Muhammad Anwar and Firsila Shah, 'Muslim Women and Experiences of Discrimination in Britain' in Jochen Blaschke (ed), *Multi-Level Discrimination of Muslim Women in Europe*, Edition Parabolis, Berlin, 2002.

Muslims and Participatory Democracy[1]

MALEIHA MALIK

Participatory democracy (defined as institutional and national identification) is important for the majority as well as the minority. However, it takes on special significance in the context of minority protection. Most obviously, minority groups whose members and viewpoints are not represented within major political and legal institutions will find it difficult to identify with them.

Institutional Identification

The relevant point for our analysis is that public institutions are not, and should not be viewed as, neutral agents. Rather they perform a wide range of functions, which influence private identity as well as political and civil society. This in turn challenges the strict separation of the private and the public sphere. It also raises questions about national identification that are discussed below. The increasing importance of 'recognition' as a political demand that characterises recent political struggles illustrates one consequence of the link between private identity and the public sphere.[2] Moreover, there are certain types of institutions that perform a critical function as a locus for private identity. They are like magnets attracting political conflict because the definitions and actions of these institutions are not just objective facts which individuals record and observe. Instead, they are matters that implicate the self-definition of citizens at a deeper level. Identification with these institutions means that individuals regard their own private identity and well being as linked with the success of the institution, and their concerns as expressed and represented within it.[3]

This vision of institutions also gives them a role that goes beyond their importance to individuals. Public institutions allow individuals to participate in shared social practices and they are a source for creating the common meanings that are a basis for community.[4] Recent Anglo-American legal theory, especially the work of Ronald Dworkin, has revived the importance of community that was a key feature of common law theory. However, the argument that certain political, legal and civic institutions are constituted by, and draw on, common meanings develops the idea of community in a much stronger form. It suggests that there are certain institutions that rely on and sustain inter-subjective meanings. These meanings can be understood by all participants and therefore contribute to the formation of a common language and vocabulary.

Common meanings and beliefs are embedded in, and constitutive of, the community: i.e. the social and political culture. These features cannot be understood by merely noting either their impact on, or their importance for, individual agents. They are not merely the shared beliefs and attitudes of an aggregate of all the individuals in a society. Rather, they form the basis for a common understanding of these social practices and institutions that cannot be understood as anything but communal. The common meanings which are associated with political, legal and civic institutions, and which they also sustain, are the basis for community. People have to share and participate in a language and understanding of norms that allow them to talk about these institutions and practices.[5] If the view that there is a stronger constitutive relationship between these institutions and private identity is accepted, then it follows that these institutions have an important function to play in creating and sustaining a political community.

Those who emphasise these constitutive features attribute an important function to institutions that goes beyond public decision-making. Certain key public institutions are also a source for constructing private behaviour and giving it meaning through the self-interpretation of participants. This complex social function assigns to these types of institutions an important role as a bank of collective wisdom and a source for 'public rituals'. Postema has made this point most forcefully in his work on Common Law:

> One might say that the processes and practices of Common Law, on this view, define a kind of secular public ritual. [...] The Common Law, then, not only defines a framework for social interaction, a set of rules and arrangements facilitating the orderly pursuit of private aims and purposes, but it also publicly articulates the social context within which the pursuit of such aims takes on meaning. It is the reservoir of traditional ways and common experience, and it provides the arena in which the shared structures of experience publicly unfold.[6]

'Institutions which identify' can be contrasted with institutions which merely 'provide a service' (e.g. a commercial organisation providing goods) and which are of purely instrumental value in the lives of citizens.[7] This is a distinction that Charles Taylor has used in his discussion of the relationship between public institutions, personal identity and national life. He argues that there is a critical connection between these concepts that has been consistently marginalised by traditional liberal theory. Taylor concludes:

> Most institutions can move along the spectrum between these extremes. Their significance may reside more or less in their function of identification; or, conversely they may slide in the direction of pure service structures.

Discussion of minority and majority issues in representative political institutions at a national and local level is an important source of generating common meanings that can be shared by both sides. It also provides a key source for developing a common language and reaching a negotiated agreement about what is 'good' for the whole community rather than 'good' for any one group. Open discussion between minorities and majorities in political institutions is a unique source for integration and social cohesion.

National Identification

The importance of institutional identification becomes even more significant when we consider that identification with the fate of a political community is also the only viable way of forming a national identity that can include minority groups. This line of argument makes it especially urgent for all minorities such as Muslims to take part in participatory democratic politics.

The traditional liberal approach constitutes the British public as members of a political community based on rational, liberal values. Citizenship identifies an unmediated relationship between individual and state: any involvement by citizens with voluntary, private or civil organisations must be voluntary and consensual. This draws upon the idea of a neutral public sphere as its essential structuring device and relegates issues of personal identity to the private sphere. The Human Rights Act (HRA) and the European Convention on Human Rights which it incorporates (ECHR) recreates this liberal 'cultural contract' by adopting a dual approach to minority protection. Its predominant concern is with the toleration of minorities, often cited as one of the main advantages of the domestic incorporation of the ECHR. Citizens are free to express their particular identity in the private sphere, either individually or in association with others, without state interference.

Contemporary strategy for the protection of minorities has supplemented toleration with a second strategy guaranteeing an individual right to non-discrimination. Although most versions of this right permit a limited measure of discrimination in the private sphere, non-discrimination ensures that minorities have access to politics, the economy and key sectors such as public services and education. This clearly affects the way in which the majority will conduct not only their private but also some of their public affairs.[8] The non-discrimination clause in Article 14 of the ECHR is limited in its application to the rights and freedoms covered by the Convention.[9] However, it has been ensured a wide application through decisions of the European Commission and European Court that confirm that there is no need to establish the violation of another article of the ECHR before Article 14 applies.[10] Moreover, the *Belgium Linguistics Case (No 2)* has affirmed that Article 14 provides some scope for positive steps to accommodate minorities: differential treatment of groups is permissible and 'equality of treatment is violated if the distinction has no objective and reasonable justification.'[11] This is in line with the European Court's recognition that democracy requires not only tolerating but also positively responding to the needs of minorities[12] Recent proposals to strengthen the ECHR's role in the protection of minorities have led to the adoption of an additional protocol which broadens the field of Article 14 to include a free standing prohibition on discrimination,[13] although this has not yet been signed by the UK.[14]

One alternative to a traditional liberal definition of political community is 'conservative nationalism' which remains a popular mechanism for defining national identity. This strategy defines the terms of belonging to a political community according to criteria such as race, common memories, a dominant culture or a majority religion.[15] In this context national identity becomes something that is given historically rather than a matter of choice or negotiation. In most Western democracies, the presence of large numbers of racially and culturally diverse groups is a permanent barrier to forging a shared national identity along the lines advocated by conservative nationalists. The fear in contemporary plural states is that the inflexible use of these criteria will necessarily exclude, or coercively assimilate, large numbers of citizens. These fears explain liberal constitutionalism's suspicion of the idea of national identity. Despite these justified reservations, anti-nationalists are coming under increasing pressure to recognise that a wide range of benefits follow from a shared national identity. It has been persuasively argued that a shared national identity minimises the risk of alienation from political institutions. It allows compromise in the face of conflicting interests; and it is a necessary pre-requisite for a politics of the common good and policies of social reform.[16]

It is against this background that a national identity as 'a sense of belonging to a political community' is advocated as the preferred concept, and one that relies on citizens identifying with the common legal and political structures in the state.[17] Even those who argue that a shared national identity is not essential accept that this 'sense of belonging to the polity' is vital for stable democratic institutions.[18] Its attraction is that it avoids the dangers of conservative nationalism whilst at the same time recognising (unlike the traditional liberal approach) that national identification performs an important function for participative democracy. Diversity (of culture, ethnicity and belief) will continue to be a problem in this context. Minorities faced with political institutions in which neither their members nor their values are adequately represented will find it difficult to view them as structures of identification. Doubts about the capacity of 'neutral' forms of governance to generate institutional identification inevitably take on a greater urgency in this context.

These doubts are exacerbated by the fact that traditional neo-liberal approaches to the protection of minorities (with their focus on toleration and non-discrimination) are increasingly seen as a necessary but insufficient policy response to the most pressing contemporary challenges to safeguarding the interests of minorities. The approach of the HRA and the ECHR to minority protection reflects the main terms of the liberal cultural contract by sustaining a neutral public sphere that avoids references to private identity such as culture, race, religion or language. The challenge posed by the politics of multiculturalism that has raged on in the 1980s and 1990s to this equilibrium has been both empirical and theoretical. These political conflicts are provoked when citizens insist on 'recognition' of their private identity (formulated on the basis of sexuality, religion or culture) in the public sphere.[19] The liberal cultural contract which relegates issues of private identity to the private sphere is not a suitable basis for responding to these demands. Theorists have increasingly questioned the adequacy of traditional liberalism's focus on universal individual rights as a sufficient guarantee for minority protection. Under conditions of ethnic or cultural diversity it is increasingly argued that concentrating exclusively on tolerance and on individual rights to non-discrimination may operate as a form of 'benign neglect' of minority groups and that multiculturalism can provide a solution.[20]

Multiculturalism, as a normative rather than descriptive term, requires policies that go beyond non-discrimination in important respects. Its concern is not limited to the protection of individuals against specific instances of discrimination but it also extends to ensuring the flourishing and survival of diverse groups (as a collective entity) within one political community.[21] Although convention rights (and the extended reading of Article 14 which permits a limited form of differential treatment) provide some scope for taking these positive steps to accommodate minorities they stop short of requiring states to 'promote the conditions necessary for persons belonging to....minorities to maintain and develop their culture and preserve the essential elements of their identity.'[22] Some forms of multiculturalism seek to address this problem by giving overwhelming priority to mechanisms of belonging which draw on the many sources of private identity (both individual and group) such as race, ethnicity or sexuality.[23] The argument is that these sources of identity should not only be tolerated in the private sphere but they should in fact be positively 'recognised' in the public sphere. Where there is a conflict between the established public or national identity and these various sources of private identity, the latter should always be given preference. This form of multiculturalism can compensate for the obvious defects of the liberal 'cultural contract' which relegates issues of personal identity to the private sphere. It also avoids the exclusionary consequences of 'conservative nationalism' that defines national identity according to historically given criteria.[24] However, seeking a solution in such an uncompromising version of multiculturalism is not free of difficulties. If participatory politics requires national identification by the minority, then this is equally true for the majority. An 'exclusive' version of multiculturalism which ignores the needs of the majority also fails to meet the criteria for an inclusive form of participatory politics.[25]

The liberal cultural contract assumes that the public sphere is a neutral space that makes no reference to issues of private identity or culture and, therefore, allows all groups to function without disadvantage. An exclusive version of multiculturalism, on the other hand, gives overwhelming priority to the accommodation of private identities of minorities within the public sphere. Both ignore the possibility that a common public sphere can emerge which is neither neutral between cultures nor a perfect mirror for personal identity.[26] This common culture will be influenced by a process of renegotiating between the diverse cultural groups within a political community. Developing 'a sense of belonging' which remains attentive to both the majority and the minority, and generating a common public culture within which different groups co-exist, requires compromise and adjustment by the parties.[27] For the minority, this means that their private identity cannot automatically be reflected in the public sphere without some limited assimilation to the shared values that are the agreed basis for a common public life.[28] For the majority, this re-negotiation carries with it significant costs. These costs will be an inevitable outcome of attempts to transform the public sphere and institutions: from exclusively reflecting the dominant culture, towards a common culture which also seeks to accommodate some of the most urgent needs of minorities.[29]

This brings the discussion back to the critical importance of institutional identification as part of a minority protection strategy. It is because citizens are more likely to identify with the decisions of representative institutions that they are an ideal forum for policies which go beyond the toleration of minorities; for example, non-discrimination policies which impact on the majority and multiculturalism. In this context, is the model of democratic politics introduced by the Human Rights Act appropriate? The idea of participation as the ability to 'trump' the majority that underlies the 'new constitutionalism' of the HRA discourse has appeal in relation to a strategy of toleration, where the aim is to safeguard certain basic rights that will provide the minimum guarantee of minority protection. It can also provide a solution to the most obvious forms of discrimination. However, this becomes less appropriate once we move beyond minimum guarantees for the toleration of minorities. Other more ambitious strategies for minority protection are likely to involve wider social redistribution of resources or renegotiations between the majority and the minority around contentious issues that require compromise by both sides. These are recurring themes in the context of certain types of indirect discrimination,[30] positive (affirmative) action or multiculturalism. The individualistic and even adversarial nature of seeing participation as control over decision-making that underlies the HRA paradigm is not inappropriate for these extended forms of minority protection. In these contexts, the ability of representative institutions to secure identification with their decisions by both the majority and the minority becomes a significant advantage. It could be argued that constitutional common law can successfully involve citizens in this project. A more expansive reading of the constitutional principle of equality and an individual right to non-discrimination have been successfully adopted to ensure that public institutions are re-structured in order to accommodate minority interests.[31] Landmark constitutional decisions such as *Brown* v *Board of Education* are usually cited as a paradigm example, confirming the ability of constitutional courts to mobilise public opinion and promote discussion on controversial issues of minority protection.[32] In this way, asserting minority interests in litigation can be a focal point for involving both the relevant minority and the majority as well as acting as a catalyst for a wider political movement.

However, in some cases, framing political issues in legally sound ways can sometimes rob them of political and purposive appeal. Michael McCann has argued that the "legal rights approach to expanding democracy has significantly narrowed their conception of political action itself" and "legal tactics not only absorb scarce resources that could be used for popular mobilization [but also] make it difficult to develop broadly based, multi-issue grassroots associations of sustained citizen allegiance".[33] In his study of US case law, Rosenberg has concluded that constitutional courts are 'constrained' when faced with litigants asking significant social reform. He argues that these are powerful constraints:

> First, they must convince the courts (or legislators) that the rights they are asserting are required by the constitutional or statutory language. Given the limited nature of constitutional rights, the constraints of legal culture, and the general caution of the judiciary this is no easy task. Second, courts are wary of stepping too far out of the political mainstream. Deferential to the federal

government and potentially limited by congressional action, courts may be unwilling to take the heat generated by politically unpopular rulings. Third, if these two constraints are overcome and cases are decided favorably, litigants are faced with the task of implementing the decisions. Lacking powerful tools to force implementation, court decisions are often rendered useless given much opposition. Even if litigators seeking significant social reform win major victories in court, in implementation they often turn out to be worth very little. Borrowing the words of Justice Jackson from another context, the Constrained Court view holds that court litigation to produce significant social reform may amount to little more than "a teasing illusion like a munificent bequest in a pauper's will".[34]

Concluding Comments

The fact that citizens are more likely to identify with the decisions of representative institutions makes them an ideal forum where minority protection policies require significant social change, re-allocation of power or resources and multiculturalism. Affirming the potential contribution of representative institutions to minority protection generally, and multiculturalism in particular, is not synonymous with displacing the well-earned and pivotal role of judicially protected individual rights for minorities. However, it is a much-needed antidote to the cherished assumption that a judicial remedy should be the sole focus of attention. Minority groups can lobby representatives to take their interests into account before formulating policies. The impact of minority protection issues on other social programmes can be considered. Policy makers can be encouraged to take into account the interests of not only minorities but also other interested parties who will be subjects of the decision when making their decisions.[35]

This is not to say that representative institutions are a panacea. Minorities such as Muslims face obvious difficulties in advancing their interests through political processes in the absence of real political power and adequate representation of their interests. Simplistic appeals to political equality leave all the most intractable difficulties unanswered in this context. 'Each citizen shall count for one' fails to account for those issues where there are individuals who are a permanent minority and whose concerns are not adequately represented within the political process. However, this speaks to the need for reform rather than abandoning the role of representative institutions altogether and a focus on transforming elected assemblies: whether at a local, regional or national level. The assumption that a judicial solution is always the first and natural option acts as a barrier to developing imaginative use of political processes by minorities to advance their interests.[36] This issue has not been explicitly or adequately addressed in the Government's constitutional reform programme,[37] which is in sharp contrast to the redistribution of power to regional assemblies ensuring that national minorities have greater control over, and are able to identify with, the political decisions which affect their daily lives.[38] The gap in the present constitutional reform agenda is also lamentable because representative institutions perform an invaluable function in minority protection. They are an ideal forum for involving all citizens and generating a debate about the appropriate balance between the needs of minorities and the wider public interest.

The argument that I have developed in this paper is that institutional identification is more likely where substantive issues concerning the common good are discussed. This in turn makes a unique contribution towards developing common meanings and a sense of community. In the context of complex plural states, I have argued that the only viable and inclusive way of defining national identification is to ensure that all citizens can identify with key political and legal institutions. This argument makes it essential that minority issues are raised in forums and at 'the point where people engage with the full range of political alternatives and the full spectrum of policy concerns'.[39] The likelihood that not only a minority such as Muslims, but also the majority will treat representative institutions as structures of identification becomes critically important for minority protection. Identification with political decisions by not only the minority but also the majority is especially important in areas of significant and controversial social reform of the public sphere. Such reform is likely to include, *inter alia*, the re-allocation of political, social and economic power from one group to another. Most importantly it will also have to provide political solutions to deep multicultural conflicts that require one group to make important concessions on key aspects of their principles or identity. Dilemmas concerning the acceptance and accommodation of Muslims in Britain often seem intractable. Many, although not all, solutions are likely to be found through the greater participation of Muslims in mainstream democratic politics.

Notes

1. This article draws on work previously published as M. Malik, 'Minority Protection and Human Rights' in Campbell, Ewing and Tomkins, *Sceptical Essays on Human Rights*. Oxford, 2002. I would like to thank the organisers and participants at the Seminar on *British Muslim: Loyalty and Belonging* at the Islamic Foundation in Leicester. I am also grateful to the following colleagues for the patient assistance with this work: Nadeem Malik, Bobby Sayyid, Tim Winter and Suhail Rahuja.
2. See Taylor, *Multiculturalism and 'The Politics of Recognition'*. Princeton University Press, USA, 1990, p. 225.
3. A. Mason, 'Political Community' in *Ethics* 261, 1999, p. 272.
4. See C. Taylor, 'Interpretation and the Sciences of Man' in *Philosophy and the Human Sciences*. Cambridge University Press, pp. 32-34. For a discussion of how legal institutions make a contribution to these goals see G. Postema, *Bentham and the Common Law Tradition*. Clarendon Press, Oxford, 1996, p. 73.
5. Ibid.
6. Postema, n. 4 above.
7. See Taylor, n. 2 above, p. 123.
8. For justifications of the anti-discrimination principle see C. McCrudden, *Anti-Discrimination Law*. Dartmouth, Aldershot, 1991.
9. Article 14 states: 'The enjoyment of the rights and freedoms set forth

in this Convention shall be secured without discrimination on any ground such as sex, race, colour, language, religion, political or other opinion, national or social origin, association with a national minority, property, birth or other status'.

10. *Grandrath* v *Federal Republic of Germany*, YBECHR 626, 1967, p. 678; *Belgium Linguistics Case (No 2)* EHRR 252, 1968.

11. Ibid p.284. Even this wider interpretation of Article 14 is a limited model to ensure the accommodation of minority cultures. In the *Belgium Linguistics Case (No 2)* the Court found that there was no general right for parents who wanted children to be educated in the language of their choice.

12. *Young, James and Webster* v *UK*, EHRR 38, 1981, p. 57. See S. Poulter, *Ethnicity, Law and Human Rights*. Oxford University Press, 1998, p.86.

13. Protocol No. 12 to the Convention for the Protection of Human Rights and Fundamental Freedoms, ETS No. 177 states: Article 1 – General prohibition of discrimination:

    (1) The enjoyment of any right set forth by law shall be secured without discrimination on any ground such as sex, race, colour, language, religion, political or other opinion, national or social origin, association with a national minority, property, birth or other status.

    (2) No one shall be discriminated against by any public authority on any ground such as those mentioned in paragraph 1. At a ceremony on 3-4 November the representatives of the member states of the Council of Europe met at the Campidoglio in central Rome to open for signature Protocol No. 12 (non-discrimination) to the ECHR.

14. A full list of signing states can be found at http://conventions.coe.int. Once 10 member states have ratified it, the Protocol will come into force, but only for ratifying states.

15. For a discussion of the intellectual roots of conservative nationalism see D. Miller, *On Nationalism*. Oxford University Press, 1995, pp. 124 - 131.

16. See A. Mason, n. 3 above and Miller, at n. 15 above, p. 237. For a detailed discussion of liberal nationalism see also Y. Tamir, *Liberal Nationalism*. Princeton University Press, 1993.

17. See Mason n.3 above and J. Habermas, 'Citizenship and National Identity: Some Reflections on the Future of Europe' in R. Beiner (ed.) *Theorising Citizenship*, SUNY Press, Albany, 1995.

18. See Mason, n. 3 above, p. 261: 'it is important nevertheless for these

states to forge and sustain a shared national identity, for they believe that in the absence of such an identity the realization of liberal values is jeopardised. In effect liberal-nationalists of this kind believe that national community is a precondition for the viability of political community as liberals conceive it.'

19. See C. Taylor, n. 2 above. See also I. M. Young, *Justice and the Politics of Difference*. Princeton University Press, 1990, pp. 163- 173.

20. For a summary of the theoretical arguments see the introduction in W. Kymlicka, *The Rights of Minority Cultures*. Oxford University Press, 1995. In the UK these issues have recently been considered in the report of the Commission on the Future of Multi-Ethnic Britain that was Chaired by Professor Lord Parekh. The Commission on the Future of Multi-Ethnic Britain was set up in January 1998 by the Runnymede Trust, an independent think-tank concerned with issues of racial justice. See http://www.runnymede trust.org/meb/ TheReport.htm for a summary of the report.

21. For a discussion of forms of multiculturalism see Miller, n. 15 above, pp. 130-141.

22. Article 4(2) of the draft Framework Convention for the Protection of National Minorities for example stated: 'The Parties undertake to adopt, where necessary, adequate measures in order to promote, in all areas of economic, social, political and cultural life, full and effective equality between persons belonging to a national minority and those belonging to the majority. In this respect, they shall take due account of the specific conditions of the persons belonging to national minorities.' As Sebastian Poulter notes, this would have provided a basis for introducing policies of multiculturalism within the ECHR structure. However, at a summit meeting held in Vienna in 1993 this draft of the protocol was not adopted. At the Vienna Meeting in 1993, the Council of Europe commissioned work on drafting a protocol in the cultural field that guaranteed individual rights of persons, especially those of national minorities. Poulter notes, 'this represented a marked shift of emphasis towards a universalist rather than a particularist approach to the issue, stressing the need to recognize the cultural rights of all rather than exclusively those of minorities.' See Poulter, n. 12 above, p. 90. For a discussion of the Council of Europe's Framework Convention for the Protection of National Minorities see P. Keller, 'Re-thinking Ethnic and Cultural Rights in Europe' *OJLS* 29, 1998.

23. See for example I. M. Young, n. 19 above, p. 167. D. Miller has described these as 'radical multiculturalism' see n. 15 above, p.135.

24. D. Miller has criticised the priority that such 'radical' forms of

multiculturalism give to affirming group difference at the expense of commonality. See n. 15 above, pp. 135 - 140.

25. Miller, n. 15 above, pp. 132 – 141.

26. Raz states that there are a number of catalysts for generating a common culture, for example, common education concerning a range of cultural groups within a society; the fact that members of all communities will interact in the same economic environment; and the fact that all cultural groups belong to the same political society. See Raz, *Ethics in the Public Domain*. Oxford University Press, 1994, pp. 188.

27. See Poulter, n. 12 above, pp. 24 – 26.

28. See Mason's justification for moderate assimilation n. 3 above, pp. 265 – 271. See also Poulter's argument, n. 12 above, that there needs to be some consensus around shared democratic values (p. 22). He also concludes that 'a culturally diverse population also requires strong elements of social cohesion around a set of shared core values, which impose certain uniform standards in the wider public interest. There are limits beyond which a tolerant attitude is inappropriate. Although such limits are hard to define with precision, they are best seen as arising from the formal, institutional values reflected in the key political and legal concepts employed in a modern liberal democracy', (p. 36).

29. See Poulter, n. 12 above, p. 34.

30. See also *Eldridge* v *British Columbia (AG)*, SCR 624, 1997 in which the Supreme Court of Canada confirmed that the failure to take positive steps to ensure that members of a disadvantaged group benefit equally from services offered to the general public (in this case the need to allocate funds to provide sign language interpreters for disabled groups) was in breach of Section 15 of the Canadian Charter of Rights and Freedoms. The Court also affirmed that this right is subject to the principle of reasonable accommodation.

31. As stated above, there is some scope for developing Art. 14 of the ECHR thereby enabling differential treatment that accommodates minority interests.

32. See for example *Brown* v *Board of Education*, US 483, 1954, or *Roe* v *Wade*, US 113, 1973.

33. Michael McCann, *Taking Reform Seriously: Perspectives on Public Interest Liberalism*. Cornell University Press, Ithaca, 1986.

34. *Edwards v California* 1941, in G. N. Rosenberg, *The Hollow Hope: Can Courts Bring About Social Change?* The University of Chicago, 1991, p. 21.

35. Poulter, n. 12 above, provides a detailed case study to show how this process can work effectively. His discussion of the events surrounding the enactment of the Construction (Head Protection) Regulations 1989 illustrate this point. Following a large number of representations from members of the Sikh community demanding an exemption (to accommodate their need to wear turbans) the Government introduced a special exemption for Sikhs. Poulter's analysis of the debates in the House of Commons and the House of Lords suggested that the decision was made after a detailed debate and after considering all the empirical evidence relating to the number of Sikh construction workers who would be effected (pp. 313 - 322).

36. For a discussion of policy options see Mason, n. 3 above and Kymlicka, n. 20 above, Part V (Minority Cultures and Democratic Theory)

37. The Labour Party Manifesto does not specifically address the issue of minority representation in its programme for reform of the House of Commons and the House of Lords, see *New Labour: Because Britain Deserves Better*. Labour Party, London, 1997. Under a section on 'Real rights for citizens' (p. 35) it refers to the incorporation of the ECHR as a source of statutory human rights; and states, 'We will seek to end unjustifiable discrimination wherever it exists. For example, we support comprehensive enforceable civil rights for disabled people against discrimination in society or at work, developed with all interested parties.' The main reference to multiculturalism is in the context of a new offence of racially motivated violence to protect ethnic minorities which resulted in the creation of racially aggravated offences in the Crime and Disorder Act 1998. See M. Malik, 'Racist Crime: Racially Aggravated Offences in the Crime and Disorder Act 1998, Part II', *MLR 409*, 1999. Recent discussions on devolution of power to regional assemblies in the northern cities provide one context for developing these ideas.

38. For a discussion of the Government's redistribution of power and the new constitutional changes see R. Brazier, 'The Constitution of the United Kingdom', *CLJ 96*, 1999.

39. A. Phillips, *The Politics of Presence*. Oxford University Press, 1995, p. 182.

Muslims in Britain: Towards a Political Agenda

S. SAYYID

Introduction

Most people have probably seen science fiction stories on TV or films where the story unfolds something like this: you are involved in an ordinary day and suddenly you enter some alternative reality or alternative universe. It looks very much like your own but it is strangely different. Recently I've been having similar experiences where I think that I have entered an alternative Universe. The event that triggered this realisation, that I was in a world which looks like ours but is not quite like ours, was an event that occurred across the Channel.

The assassination of Pim Fortuyn, an ex-Marxist Sociology Professor, an Islamophobe and, of course, the leader of a Dutch political party was this event. Pim Fortuyn was killed by a vegetarian. However, what struck me as being particularly extraordinary about this event was that I was able to watch and listen to interviews with Muslims who wept and mourned the death of a self-confessed Islamophobe. A charitable way of looking at this would be to say that these Muslims were mourning the fact that a human being died and no one actually rejoices in such a case. I suppose a more cynical way of looking at it would be to assume that Muslim organisations put the wreaths out for purely opportunistic reasons. After all, politics is grown-up stuff. We all do things that require a little dissimulation, a little twisting of the truth, and maybe Muslim organisations in the Netherlands thought it politically advantageous to be among Pim Fortuyn's mourners.

The really terrifying thought was that this was not an act of political calculation but, rather, a genuine act of mourning. I'm not saying there should be dancing on his grave, but it seemed to me that a dignified silence should have sufficed. Why was it that these people felt compelled to somehow demonstrate their mourning for the passing of someone who had little respect for their faith or heritage? It is this question that I wish to explore. I want to take seriously the possibility that the Muslim mourning of Fortuyn's assassination was not mainly a matter of political calculation but rather a genuine response to murder. The question, though, is why?

Why is it that Muslims in the Netherlands felt compelled to somehow mourn the loss of someone who condemned them, who did not really want them to be Muslims, who said you were welcome to be in the Netherlands but you must 'integrate'; that is, cease to be a Muslim in any meaningful sense.

Muslims and Politics

The primary political question is always who are our friends and who are our enemies. It is this distinction between friend and enemy that determines the political itself. Politics is only partly about having politicians or councillors or MPs of particular interest. Fundamentally politics is the process by which who we are and who we are going to be is made manifest. It is the process of identification that is inherently political. Who are our friends and who are our enemies? It is through answering these question that we come to a sense of ourselves. Without enemies there can be no value to being a friend. A world in which we cannot distinguish between friends and enemies is a world without the political. A world without the political is a world in which existing power relations are considered to be natural and uncontested, a world without the political is also a world in which we cannot dream of something different let alone something better.

The assertion of an Islamicate political identity means that being Muslim begins to mean something other than observing the rituals and practices of Islam. It means that one tries to read from being a Muslim, one's social and political obligations. Being a Muslim requires an engagement with the rest of the *ummah*; it would be difficult to imagine how one could be a Muslim without regard to the rest of the *ummah*. This ummatic component of Muslim identity is precisely where Muslims come into contact with authorities of the Westphalian state – since a Muslim identity transcends the boundaries of the nation-state. Hence, the figure of the Muslim has become symptomatic of the crisis of the nation-state. It is not mere coincidence that the emergence of Islamophobia in Europe seems to go hand in hand with the articulation of a pan-European identity.

Attempts to deny the Ummatic dimension of an Islamicate political identity are varied. Many come from Muslims themselves – often presenting themselves as being 'moderate'. (What does it mean to be 'moderate' in the face of cruelty and injustice?) It also comes from those governments and organisations who would like to 'nationalise' Islamicate identity. Even the Runnymede Trust Report on Islamophobia suggests that Muslims should not involve themselves in issues outside Britain (especially the Middle East) oddly; the Runnymede Trust Report on anti-Semitism does not offer this advice to the Jewish community. The nationalisation of Islamicate identity is often the first step in producing a secularised vision of Islam, in which it becomes reduced to an exotic exhibition along with saris and steel bands.

The model that most of the Islamist groups (for example, the Muslim Brotherhood, Jama'at-e-Islami) have deployed up to now has been, to some extent, influenced by the success of the vanguardist parties in Europe during the 1920s and 1930s. The Vanguard party saw itself as an elite, whose role was to lead and direct the masses. But the party was not of the masses and it maintained its distinction from them. The Bolshevik party provides a paradigmatic example of such an approach to political organisation. The aim of the Vanguard party was to use the disciplined cadres of the party to storm the structures of the state, and once the state was captured it would be possible to use the power of the state to bring about social transformation. This is the pattern that Gramsci analysed as being the 'war of manoeuvre'. He contrasted this with what he called a 'war of position'. In this strategy power is gained by cultural and intellectual reform. An example of a successful 'war of position' is provided by the feminist movement, which, in a space of thirty years, managed to transform the position of women throughout the world, without ever capturing state power.

The political position of Muslims in Britain does not depend on the number of Muslim MPs, or local councillors. Currently, there are four or five parliamentarians and perhaps over 200 local councillors. It is often assumed that having more Muslims in various public forums of Britain would be of benefit to Muslims in Britain in general. I think, however, that this assumption is somewhat naïve as Muslim representation often comes with a price tag. Muslim representatives risk being incorporated into the mainstream, rather than representing Muslim interests. Recent examples include the way in which Muslim parliamentarians were marshalled into supporting the war against Afghanistan – a war that the overwhelming majority of Muslims and many non-Muslims opposed.

Islamicate Political Identity and Muslim Interests

Ultimately, it seems to me that representation only makes sense in a context in which there is a minimum agenda which Muslims can sign up to and thus insist that their representatives (Muslim or non-Muslim) are identified by the advocacy of the agenda. Currently, it is not clear what the involvement of Muslims in public affairs means. What is common to the experience of Muslims in Britain, apart from Islamophobia? In other words, we can say that Muslims are commonly subject to regulation and discrimination and other forms of social exclusion, but even in that area we can argue that there is a huge difference depending on class background, educational achievements etc. Nor can it be decisively argued that there is anything specific about these aspects of social exclusion. By and large, many of these problems are faced by other members of ethnically marked populations in Britain. (It should be borne in mind, that many recent reverts to Islam do become ethnically marked as a result of their reversion.) Does being a member of a Muslim community in Britain mean that we stand for anything? That is, do Muslims have any enemies, and do they have any friends?

What, if any, are common areas of concern? How do we actually manifest any kind of agenda, and how can we actually build something? There is perhaps one area in which most Muslims in Britain have a similar position and that is the critique of Zionism as most Muslims support the Palestinian cause. If we could extend this kind of consensus to more issues then we would be in a situation similar to the feminist movement in that a diffuse set of political activists separated along a variety of dimensions are able to make coherent political demands without the necessity of obvious central leadership. What this means is that Muslims have to engage in the process of building consensus (like the one around the critique of Zionism and support of the Palestinian people) over a longer list of issues. Some of these issues may be foreign policy issues and others maybe domestic. If we could struggle for these key issues

(Kashmir, Chechnya, de-colonisation of the British state, greater social and economic equality etc.) so that Muslims (and non-Muslims) could recognise in these issues the interest and identity of the Muslim community. This would be a far greater guarantee of a Muslim presence in public affairs than would an increase in the number of individual Muslim 'representatives' in parliament or the media. It is not the presence of individual Muslims, but a distinct and independent Muslim voice that will guarantee for Muslims a position beyond Islamophobia.

I would like to conclude this series of rather disjointed reflections by making two main points. First, there is no doubt that the main way that a European identity is being increasingly defined is by the exclusion of Muslims. The various anti-immigrant and anti-ethnic minority groups are increasingly liable to deny their racism but accept their Islamphobia. For example, the BNP makes a distinction between Asians and Muslims. Asians, they will concede (at least publicly), can become part of British cultural formation, but Muslims can only become British by abandoning their commitment to the *ummah*, by 'modernising' their system of beliefs - in short by ceasing to be Muslims. Thus, the problem of Islamophobia is not likely to diminish until the problem of a pan-European identity is itself resolved. This means addressing issues such as what does it actually mean to be European, how would Europe change as a result of recognising the Muslim presence in its midst? I would suggest Muslims should be wary of the attempt to articulate a distinct "European Islam" in which Islam is subsumed within a European identity, for while such an operation suggests an end to Islamophobia, it does so at the expense of the existence of Islam as a distinct way of life. This means that the Muslim presence has to become more openly associated with a critique of a way of thinking which considers European values to be universal and intrinsically superior. In other words, the articulation of a distinct Muslim subjectivity cannot be separated from a deepening of the process of de-colonisation.

My second main point is a question of strategy. How do Muslims in Britain move from our current situation to a better one? I realise strategies are easy to formulate in the abstract but difficult to implement in the concrete. Despite this, it maybe useful to have some kind of pointers as to what course of action Muslims could fruitfully pursue.

Thus, as I have suggested before, what Muslims need is a 'war of position', that is, a model of political action similar to that of the feminist movement. Muslims must confront the problem of trying to bring about a transformation in cultural practices in situations in which their presence is fragmented, in which they lack a plausible central leadership.[1] The first move towards a 'war of position' is to develop a narrative which links these different issues, that affect different Muslims, together. Muslims do not need to speak with one voice, but it would be helpful if they draw upon one big story that could account for their current condition both in Britain and the rest of the world. The advantage of such a story would be that they would not have to rely on intrinsically Islamophobic narratives for explaining their situation. Such a story would help Muslims distinguish between their friends and their enemies. At the very least it would explain why we do not need to mourn, except as mark of respect for common humanity, the death of an Islamophobe. Muslims have to try and move the debate to a ground where you can actually have a dialogue, rather than a monologue which pretends to be a debate, where Muslims are expected to answer questions based on the assumptions that already defeat their position. Muslims of Britain need to stitch together a narrative, in which individual stories will become part of a larger tapestry, to recognise that the problems they face are not purely autobiographical but structural. To recognise that a Muslim community is not contained within the limits of this island, that we are a global community, that we have a global heritage (and that it is a source of our strength), and that we do not need to speak simply as supplicants, either to government or to European cultural formation. It is possible for us to have a dialogue as equals, and therefore, when an exchange takes place, it takes place as equals. This is why we have to abandon those narratives that try to place us in positions of inferiority. We have to abandon the discourse of Western supremacy that has held sway for perhaps five hundred years.

Conclusion

I would like to suggest that the problem of Islamophobia cannot simply be addressed by a greater representation of 'Muslims' in key institutions and structures without the reform of those institutions and structures. Such representation without reform risks producing more Muslim Islamophobes. Having more Muslims in higher echelons of the media, government or academia would only make a difference if these Muslims behaved in a way that did not simply reproduce institutional Islamophobia and racism which is inherent in large sections of British society. A political agenda for Muslims in Britain cannot be separated from a demand for a deeper process of decolonisation. For it is only by decolonising the narrative which fixes European identity as superior and others as inferior, that Muslims can establish themselves outside the framework of Islamophobia.

Notes

1. For a variety of reasons I don't think that the Muslim community in Britain should centralise itself within one leadership figure, partly because I think that the risks of such a leadership being incorporated into British establishment are very great.

Discussion

YAHYA BIRT: How much detail concerning religious affiliation is going to be recorded in the Census results?

Given that the question on religious affiliation was voluntary, this information may be quite limited although there have been recommendations put forward and pressure groups have been lobbying for more information with regards to people's religious affiliations. This is in fact an area where Muslims should continue to lobby. This information is not just important to Muslims. Local councils and other service providers would need to know what proportion of local populations are Muslim. As the census is the most reliable source for population figures that is the best way of collecting data on religion, rather than relying on much smaller surveys.

DAUD MATHEWS: You referred to the need for more Muslims to be involved in the media, perhaps one solution might be for each mosque or centre to appoint a media officer? As for the figures of Muslims in Parliament, could this under-representation not be compensated for by lobbying or pressure groups initiated or supported by the outreach work of organisations like TELCO?

MUHAMMAD ANWAR: *Muslim MP's do not represent Muslims only as they are elected by a whole constituency, but at least as individuals Muslims are getting involved in the political process* *because, if you are not there then you are not part of the process. We are talking about sharing power, therefore, it is important who is there. Some Muslim representatives could actually be harmful to the Muslim cause. I would agree that a lobby by Muslims is needed and would also agree with the idea of some form of media representation.*

ZAHID PARVEZ: A Rabbi once addressed a predominantly Christian audience and informed them that the Jewish community had reached the heights of power in Britain within one generation. This was achieved despite facing very similar problems to those experienced by the Muslim community. What prevents Muslims from replicating this example? Is this process really hindered simply by prejudice?

MUHAMMAD ANWAR: *Although there may be some similarities in the experiences of first generation migrants, Eastern European Jews are racially similar to their European counterparts and within one generation integration took place because Jews could not, on the whole, be racially identified as being 'other'. The Jewish population is steadily decreasing unlike the Muslim population which is increasing. Discrimination is based largely on race and culture as well as religion and colour. So while there are similarities, there are also marked differences between the Muslim and Jewish communities.*

SEAMUS MARTIN: You quoted figures for Christian and Muslims from the census information, comparing like with like, but what is the definition of a Muslim? Is it based on ethnic origins or religious affiliation?

MUHAMMAD ANWAR: *The calculations of Muslims in Britain are based on their country of origin and ethnic origins. It would be a mistake to compare figures of so-called 'practising' religious entities. How much or how little people practise their faith is irrelevant in these calculations although the question of 'religious affiliation' inclusion in the census might show a more accurate figure of people who define themselves by their religious identity.*

FAIYAZUDDIN AHMED: Muslims in Britain are not a homogenous entity and, therefore, unity on many issues is hard to achieve although there are some points of convergence. This fractionalisation may be due to the fact that most Muslims originate from other countries and therefore this divergence of opinion will, therefore, last for many years, but this diversity can possibly be an advantage.

MUHAMMAD ANWAR: *The Jews have many varying and differing opinions amongst themselves and this is apparent from reading their newspapers yet they are able to come together and reach an agreement on matters of national and international importance. Muslims likewise should work towards a united view if not united front.*

Session Four: **Open Forum and Looking Ahead**

Open Forum and Looking Ahead

IBRAHIM HEWITT: When the media reports on Muslims in Parliament they are always reported in terms of their religion. For example Muhammad Sarwar MP, is usually portrayed as, 'the Muslim MP'. As mentioned, the feminist movement has made great advances in the political sphere in terms of participation and representation and they make a good example of how Muslims might make advances into the political arena. How do Muslims get to this level of involvement?

MALEIHA MALIK: *The feminist model is a good example but it entails more than just being a woman. What do we mean when we say someone is a Muslim MP and how do we judge what makes them a Muslim? We need to develop a single narrative or view on specific important issues affecting us as a community, like the narrative on Palestine that is largely shared by all Muslims. Political representation can be exampled by the Sex Discrimination Act, by which there are proposed 'all women short-lists'. The analogy is that women can be specifically preferred and chosen for representation and election to increase the number of women present in parliament. However, the aspect of accountability is an important one, all the more so when applied to the case of Muhammad Sarwar for example. Ideas and strategies need to be generated which represent so form of consensus in terms of Muslim concerns and issues.*

YAHYA BIRT: Young Muslim activists have been directly influenced by the anti-globalisation movement and peace movements since 2001, with respect to organisations and tactics, rather than the feminist movement. It is more important to start the discussion with a consideration of how these activists have chosen to engage politically, rather than by making more speculative analogies.

S. SAYYID: *Analogies and models are problematic. For example comparing our situation with the Jews and their apparent commonalties with Muslims – why can't we replicate their successes? It is because our circumstances are different. The feminist model represents a similarity because, firstly, they have attained a form of diffused power without a single voice, and secondly, they have managed to change the frame of reference. However, the difference with the feminist struggle is that it neither questioned nor challenged Western hegemony. It just wanted to participate in the political process. Equally, being a woman in power, for example Margaret Thatcher, does not make you a feminist. Likewise, a Muslim MP represents the same dilemma, particularly if he is supporting the government in the bombing of Afghanistan. But the idea of a diffused movement that can find representation and evoke change is a useful example for Muslims.*

FATMA AMER: Unfortunately, the notion of 'common good' for many Muslims does not extend beyond the confines of their own community but perhaps once the practicalities and realities of what it means to 'belong' are discussed and understood then strategies and programmes for participation can be addressed. This is a natural course of events that will take time.

HISHAM AL-ZOUBEIR: UK legislation is way behind European legislation against discrimination and I cannot see Muslims pushing for reform of British laws regarding the European Convention on Human Rights.

MALEIHA MALIK: *The British government has not yet implemented Protocol Twelve of the European Convention on Human Rights and I have been reliably informed that the British Government has no intention at the present time of doing so. This does not mean that it will not implement it in the future but already civil rights activists and trade unionists are pushing for its implementation. Laws tackling xenophobia, racial and religious hatred need to be extended to protect religious minorities like Muslims. Furthermore, Muslims represent a significant minority at the European level and they should be aware of this and exercise this power by forming alliances and lobbies within the European Parliament. Once participation and representation has been established at European level, this will have a massive impact at national level.*

The 'little Englander' and anti-European mentality is an inhibitor in the process of social inclusion and integration in Britain. Muslims should be aware of the developments in Europe where states appoint and patronise a national representation for Muslim communities, similar to the Church Synod. We should evaluate the implications of state-sponsored governing religious bodies.

REV. ANDREW WINGATE: The British National Party's anti-Muslim political campaign, which is aimed at increasing tensions and hostilities between Muslims and Hindus and Sikhs, has been stepped-up in locations where there are large ethnic communities. In my area vicious tapes have been circulated to people of other faiths; the local council advised that we should ignore them as the BNP simply wanted more publicity. In response, our local interfaith group organised a 'solidarity' meeting which was attended by well over one hundred people and in Leicester imams take the time to talk to Christian groups which opens up the discourse towards understanding. What can and should be done to combat this Islamophobic, anti-Muslim sentiment?

S. SAYYID: *It is interesting in regard to this problem that when Muslims do something good and valuable, it is in spite of Islam and when they do something bad or evil it is because of Islam. The historical understanding of Muslims in the West fits into the framework of the Judeo-Christian tradition. The history of the West from Plato to NATO excludes the contribution of Islam. A new narrative for telling the history of the world has to be developed. It is important to understand the existing narrative is an inherited model from colonalisation that assumes there is only one valid cultural formation and nothing else. There are, of course, different historical roots and different historical interpretations. Today, however, we start with the assumption that there is only one history and nothing else – this is something that needs to be broken down.*

FAIYAZUDDIN AHMAD: From Professor Anwar's paper, we see that 60 per cent of Muslims in Britain were born here and they now represent the second and third generations. I am from the remaining 40 per cent. But I was born a British subject in India where it became unsafe for me and my parents to reside so we sought sanctuary in the then East Pakistan. We learned the language, the customs and the culture but eventually we were told that we were not loyal and so we had to leave. We made our way to England nineteen years ago. Now again I am asked are you loyal and do you belong to this country? My only solace comes from the Qur'ān, (the verses about loyalty to God and his Prophet), and the fact that I, as a Muslim, am not compelled to do anything which contravenes this. Tebbit has his cricket matches and Blunkett his language tests, but we have known English since childhood – are we not British? I don't know the answer to this, but what I do know is that if I contribute to the good and well-being of this society then I am performing my religious duty.

BATOOL AL-TOMA: Professor Muhammad Anwar's statistics on Muslims in Britain are based on names and ethnic origins and this presents a problem as many non-Arabic sounding names, such as those of many Turks, do not indicate that they are Muslim. As a convert to Islam, I am a minority within a minority and many of my convert brothers and sisters do not have 'Muslim' names. Surely Muslims are defined by their beliefs and practices and, therefore, to identify Muslims by their names or ethnic origins must be increasingly problematic. Furthermore, how seriously can we lobby for Muslim rights when, particularly after September 11th, Muslim women were noticeably absent from the political arena. Because women represent at least 50 per cent of the Muslim population without their participation, how valid is the present political representation?

MALEIHA MALIK: *Statistics are the key basis on which resources and funds are allocated. Recommendations are being addressed for the new census. The need for local authorities to locate the number of Muslims in their boundaries is apparent and this deems the tracing of Muslims simply by their names or ethnic origins as somewhat inaccurate. But, for the moment, using names is the best tool that we have, as Professor Anwar explained. The issues concerning Muslim women are here to stay and the main critique of Islam is the status afforded to women by Muslims. We need to retrieve an important tradition regarding the real place of our women. Research of early Muslim history and civilisation clearly shows the full participation of women in all spheres of life. The fight is on two fronts: changing Muslim attitudes and non-Muslim perceptions. Therefore, the challenge is to address these issues.*

MOHAMMAD SIDDIQUE SEDDON: I have a question by way of seeking practical advice from our Christian brother, Rev. Andrew Wingate. The representation of British Muslims is somewhat disparate because of the various expressions of Islam present and therefore finding a shared narrative, like that of the feminists, is difficult. Despite similar difficulties of sectarianism,

Christian denominations have worked together to form umbrella organisations by which their religious interests can be represented. How can British Muslims achieve similar progress?

REV. ANDREW WINGATE: This achievement is really part of a historical development that has seen Anglicanism and Catholicism come together. It was only fifty years ago that these two Christian denominations could not offer the Lord's Prayer together. But Christians have been largely able to put their differences aside for the sake of working for the shared common good. I suppose it is still early days for Muslims and it can be a long process in which differences must be put aside in order to come closer. This was achieved by Christians on two levels, at the local or grass roots, finding commonalties and at a high level within the Church leadership. The Vatican Council opened-up the theological dialogue. British Muslims have political representation like the Federation of Muslim Organisations in Leicestershire or the Muslim Council of Britain in London but this does not seem to represent the religious body of Muslims. The Council of Mosques and Imams is perhaps a solution. But because Muslims do not have a clergy, it is sometimes difficult to know whom to deal with. I suppose working together through structures is one way and the historical influence of the Church can help Muslims.

SEAN McLOUGLIN: My question is for Salman Sayyid concerning the 'common good'. The notion of shared boundaries and civic culture in the discourse of multiculturalism within the context of structural relationships, presented by lobbies, of minority and majority entities, points to the need for a new narrative for British Muslims. Also the idea of European identity being defined in opposition to Islam. What do you think of this new emphasis on the common good and shared values? Is there any mileage in it? Does it inevitably mean the hegemony of one over the other? This is what was being said in the 1980's, that shared culture is just a new way of re-articulating the hegemonic culture. Parekh, talks about the procedural boundaries of specific cultures and communities being left of centre. Others speak of multi-relating and multi-cultural convergence. Where do you position yourself in this debate amongst the newly developing competing visions?

S. SAYYID: *I am critical of the notion of the common good. It is all very well until things get difficult. After September 11, for example 1,500 Muslims were imprisoned for twenty-three days in the United States for reasons they were not at all sure of. At what point does the shared notion of the common good, the kind of benign getting together and living in harmony like the coca-Cola song, fragment? The content of this culture is designed very specifically and it is defined hegemonically. However, the danger in it is certain areas are conceded, like food or clothes, but not in substantive issues of policy, so that multiculturalism is reduced to multi-cuisine. The Muslim narrative has to be a global one and not just about Muslims but about the whole world. Like that of Palestine – all Muslims agree on the issues. The Muslim narrative has to be historical and cannot simply be based around taking certain notions of the common good because those notions are described in very specific national and cultural contexts. They are exclusionary of certain ways of thinking and Muslims have always traditionally challenged this limited idea of loyalty and belonging. For example, Enoch Powell considered himself to be English because his ancestors fought at the Battle of Waterloo. Muslim identity does not fit well into the dominant description of national and ethnic belonging. A Muslim identity disrupts that and this is why the notions of common good are not going to be very helpful. We have to put this imposed idea of the common good against the story that Muslims tell of themselves and their place in the world, past, present and future.*

MALEIHA MALIK: *I disagree with Salman. I believe it is not possible nor advisable for Muslims to reject the notion of a common good. Parekh wants to make a subjectivist argument about culture and notions of the common good. Definitions of law in Islam, what we call the* Maqāṣid as-Sharī'ah, *or the commentary of Ghazālī's interpretation of politics and law offer an articulation of certain objective goods which are universal and always have been true in time. They are goods for all human beings to pursue. This is where you get the link, the narrative from which Muslims can distinguish themselves from the slide into subjectivism that is the hall-mark of the debates around multiculturalism at the moment. This is what is distinctive about the contributions we make. In terms of the common good, it does not mean we cannot form links, but we have got a very distinctive truth to communicate about the sense of the common good and the way in which one has access to it. For example Ghazālī defines these as being: family, wealth, dignity, health, faith etc. Now what is striking about this is that it provides the link with the other universal narrative traditions and revealed religions, Judaism and Christianity. A parallel reading of Ghazālī's and Aquinas' legal theory shows striking parallels, a shared language about the role of natural law and the role of the common good that man has to pursue. This is the contribution that all religious traditions have to make to the contemporary world in the context of modernity. This idea of the common good is critical to who we are as individuals and a community, and what our narrative is.*

S. SAYYID: *It is fine to disagree but it is important to know what we disagree about. It is clear that the operation of the common good has a very clear enlightenment signature rather than a Christian signature. It is difficult to break the link with Christianity but it is more of an enlightenment signature than anything else. Secondly, it seems to me that one has to recognise that all of these things are historical. What is not historical is the*

Qur'ān, but the rest is historical commentary which actually reflects certain conditions and times. We may want to have a conversion with al-Ghazālī and our past but it does not seem to me that they are anything other than historical. Once you start talking in terms of 'revealed religion' you still have a problem – what do you do about Buddhism or atheism? It is very easy to have a cosy 'Abrahamic cousins together' kind of arrangement. What we are talking about here is a common good that extends this discourse and is perhaps more to do with notions of the secular which is actually important to the common good. This is of course slightly problematic – I am not sure what a secular Muslim would be like! Nevertheless, leaving aside all these issues, the point is not that Muslims do not have a contribution to make to the common good. Rather, that when al-Ghazālī talks about family, wealth, it may be that such terms could also be used in other terms – maintaining a system which is iniquitous in terms of social wealth and distribution. There are many different meanings that one could have from these principles and therefore it does not really tell us a great deal. The notion that you could simply have an agreement on procedures and that in itself would be sufficient would be ideal if it were correct. However, the problem is that all procedures are embedded in cultural practices that actually give them their definition. Furthermore, the problem with cultural practices is that there is a demand to have ownership over them because they are a privilege in certain circumstances. That is why when the US talks about a war against terrorism and then begins ethnic profiling, it does not say that these are American Muslims and that they have every right as does any other group. At the same time they have Hamza Yusuf acting as a Muslim Advisor to President Bush whilst the FBI is raiding his house for being a Muslim! These are not just anomalies of the system; it is actually quite fundamental. What kind of a Muslim can you be in the case of the US when to question the current government policy becomes almost tantamount to treason? It is these types of issues that surface when a Muslim says his supreme loyalty is to God, and through that to the Muslim Ummah, *that when the state says that your loyalty has to be solely to the state against any other possibilities. In addition, when you have, for example, the Editor of the* National Review Online *saying, 'Let's nuke Makkah (sic)' – how are Muslims supposed to respond by saying, 'Yeah! Good idea! My country right or wrong'? I do not think we can do that! These are the issues when it really comes to the crunch. That is why we need to have a narrative that is global, because the narrative we are confronted with, that makes all of these things fit together and presents them as plausible, is also global.*

SHER KHAN: My observation is that the nature of our discussions so far has largely been about 'us' and 'them' in terms of ourselves and the policyholders, representation and power brokering. I would like us to return to the notions of loyalty and belonging in the context of citizenship. Perhaps one of the mechanisms by which we can feel a sense of belonging to an identity is if we feel we are involved in shaping this identity. There are many discussions in which we can contribute, such as the debate on citizenship. There is no contradiction between loyalty to God and the state. Tebbit's extreme definitions of loyalty represent for most people a form of exclusive nationalism, which most people would reject.

SARAH JOSEPH: The concept of citizenship, away from the international and national definitions, is perhaps more about my neighbours and the local community. The Muslim understanding of the common good should not be a parochial one; rather it should be about the whole of humanity. Therefore, a Muslim should not only ask, 'Is this good for me?' The question is, 'Is it good for humanity?'

KHALIL REHMAN: The key element in implementing change is education. 60 per cent of Muslims in Britain live in the south east with the other 40 per cent dispersed elsewhere throughout the country. The battle seems to be on two fronts, firstly, with ourselves and our own representation and secondly, formulating a coherent discourse. Muslim representatives at the present are largely born outside the UK and their concerns appear to be primarily economic. With regard to Muslims in the US it would seem that their loyalty and belonging leads to being locked-up without reason – is that what comes of being loyal? In terms of our full participation as citizens through social and political inclusion, it is a matter of legislation changes through lobbying and persistence.

MALEIHA MALIK: *It was very sad to see the Muslim leadership capitulating and standing 'shoulder to shoulder' with the Prime Minister when that was the time to negotiate for our needs. It was then that we could have pushed for legislation and social change in return for supporting the government.*

S. SAYYID: *But support the government at what cost? Two groups historically suffered as a result of assimilation: the Jews in Germany and the Muslims in Bosnia. These examples are a warning. Another dimension is the aspect of being a 'minority'. This status would only apply if you believed in hermetically sealed boundaries. Any such boundaries have been eroded and made irrevocably irrelevant by globalisation. Muslims are not a minority they are a large presence on this planet. This trans-national nexus is very important to us. In this context the problem with making a 'deal' with the government would mean that, when you are asked to support the war on terrorism in exchange for possible legislation, you may find yourself trading in the blood of other Muslims. We have to ask 'Do we want such legislation on these terms?' If we accept this type of 'deal', what kind of Muslims would we be? It is paramount that we are cautious and that we remain true to our religious principles.*

MALEIHA MALIK: *Very briefly, I wish people had taken this stance. I respect this principled approach. However, within the present leadership, there are perhaps too many who have compromised without achieving any results – the worst of both worlds! In the final analysis we need to understand the political process and then fully participate in it to achieve the desired results; in short, be more strategically political.*

Contributors Profiles

MUHAMMAD ANWAR is Research Professor at the Centre for Research in Ethnic Relations (CRER) University of Warwick, having formerly been Director of CRER (1989-94) and Head of Research, Commission for Racial Equality (1982-89). He has written extensively on ethnic and race relations.

IMTIAZ AHMAD HUSSAIN is a graduate of Islamic Studies and Arabic language, Institute of Islamic Research, Al-Azhar University, Cairo, and a Member of the Organising Committee of the International Leadership Training Programme, Da'wah Academy, International Islamic University, Islamabad. He is a qualified social worker, specialising in training and mentoring and is currently completing his postgraduate studies in Arabic translation at the Department of Middle Eastern Studies, University of Manchester. He has vast experience in youth and community work in both the voluntary and statutory sectors and is presently employed as the Co-ordinator for the Manchester Islamic Schools Trust.

NEIL JAMESON is the Executive Director of The Citizen Organising Foundation. He built the UK's first broad based community organisation in Bristol in 1989 and was invited to east London to build a similar alliance in the capital in 1994. Prior to helping establish COF Neil Jameson worked for 'The

Childrens Society' and 'Save the Children' in both the south west of England and several northern cities. He opened and developed one of the first Family Centres in the UK in Coventry in 1976. He qualified as a social worker in 1971. He is a Quaker, married to Jean, a teacher and with a family of four children. He has travelled extensively working in the Sudan and USA and visiting India, Bangladesh and eastern Europe to study civil society.

MALEIHA MALIK has been a lecturer in Law at the School of Law, King's College, London, since 1993. Her research interests include Tort, Discrimination Law and Jurisprudence. She regularly publishes on minority rights and racially aggravated crime. *Faith and Law* (Hart Publications, 2000) features among her recent publications.

S. SAYYID is a Lecturer at the University of Salford. His research interests include: post-structuralist political thought, Islamism and Eurocentrism and early state structures. He is the author of *A Fundamental Fear: Eurocentrism and the Emergence of Islamism* (Zed Books, 1997) and is a member of the Executive Committee of the Association of Muslim Social Scientists.

TIM WINTER was in born 1960 and educated at Westminster School and Pembroke College, Cambridge. He was appointed Lecturer in Islamic Studies, Faculty of Divinity, University of Cambridge, in 1997. He is also a Fellow and Director of Studies in Theology at Wolfson College, Cambridge, Member of the Board of Management for Middle Eastern and Islamic Studies, Faculty of Oriental Studies also at Cambridge. In addition he is a Member of the Management Committee, Centre of Islamic Studies, School of Oriental and African Studies, London, and is the Academic Liaison Officer, Thesaurus Islamicus Foundation in Liechtenstein. His publications include *Al-Ghazālī on Death* (1989), *Al-Ghazālī on Disciplining the Soul* (1995), and several articles on Islamic theology.

List of Participants

Dr Manazir Ahsan, *The Islamic Foundation*
Dr Fatma Amer, *Markfield Institute of Higher Education*
Professor Muhammad Anwar, *University of Warwick*
Dr Mehmet Asutay, *University of Leicester*
Umar Best, *Leeds*
Wakila Best, *Leeds*
Yahya Birt, *Forum Against Islamophobia and Racism*
Ian Byrne, *Cuddesdon Theological College*
Susi Calder, *Citizens in the West Midlands*
Dr Abdel Kader Chachi, *The Islamic Foundation*
Margaret Cooper, *London*
Dr Seif el-Din Tag el-Din, *Markfield Institute of Higher Education*
Syed Faiyazuddin, *The Islamic Foundation*
Ian Fletcher, *University of Manchester*
Ilyas Foy, *Burnley College*
Ibrahim Hewitt, *al-Aqsa School, Leics.*
Dilwar Hussain, *The Islamic Foundation*
Imtiaz Ahmad Hussain, *Muslim Schools Trust, Manchester*
Neil Jameson, *Citizen Organising Foundation*
Brunel Jones, *Diocese of Bradford*
Sarah Joseph, *The Muslim Council of Britain*
Sher Khan, *The Muslim Council of Britain*
Keith Littlejohn, *Cuddesdon Theological College*
Ibrahim Longden, *Stockport City Council*

Maleiha Malik, *King's College London*
Nadeem Malik, *Citizen Organising Foundation*
Seamus Martin, *Freelance Lecturer*
Daud Matthews, *International Council for Islamic Information*
Dr Sean McLoughlin, *University of Leeds*
Dominic Mogul, *Diocese of Bradford*
Farooq Murad, *The Islamic Foundation*
Zahid Parvez, *University of Wolverhampton*
Khalil Rehman, *The Islamic Society of Britain*
Atia Rifat, *The Islamic Society of Britain*
Rev. Angus Ritchie, *Citizen Organising Foundation*
Adil Salahi, *Markfield Institute of Higher Education*
S. Sayyid, *University of Salford*
Khadija el-Shayyal, *The Young Muslims UK*
Mohammad Siddique Seddon, *The Islamic Foundation*
Dr Ataullah Siddiqui, *Markfield Institute of Higher Education*
Batool al-Toma, *The New Muslims Project*
Rev. Andrew Wingate, *Interfaith Advisor to the Bishop of Leicester*
Tim Winter, *University of Cambridge*
Chowdhury Mueen Uddin, *The Islamic Foundation*
Faraz Yousafzai, *Young Citizens in the West Midlands*
Hisham al-Zoubeir, *University of Warwick*